Nothing to Declare

Nothing to Declare

A Memoir

Taki

THE ATLANTIC MONTHLY PRESS
NEW YORK

For Alexandra, Mandolyna and John-Taki

*This book could not have been written without the
help of Lenora De Sio.*

First published in Great Britain in 1991 by Viking
First Atlantic Monthly Press edition, June 1991
Printed in the United States of America

ISBN 0-87113-484-5
Library of Congress card number 91-10724

The Atlantic Monthly Press
19 Union Square West
New York, NY 10003

First printing

· *Preface* ·

It's impossible to be lonely in Southampton during the sparkling summer months, especially if you happen to own a spacious house with swimming pool, tennis court and a cellarful of wine, and have a courteous staff in attendance. Southampton, for the benefit of anyone who has spent the last fifty years in Albania, is the luminous little village in Long Island which serves as seaside refuge for New York's civilized rich during the unbearable heat of urban summer. As full of socialites as it is free of socialists, Southampton has been described by the glossy magazines that describe such places as an antiseptic, overrefined backwater of grand houses, wicker chairs, yellow and white umbrellas and long green lawns.

It is, of course, much more than that, the more being the people who live in the grand houses. For a few glorious months each year, they create a community which might be the nearest we will get, in this forlorn age, to the country-house culture that the English gave to the world and once seemed the only way to live. No doubt this, too, will be extinguished by the unsparing barbarism of modern life. Southampton falls into the category of things governed by what I call, in the appropriate parlance, the First Law of Sociodynamics. Any social tradition which depends for its survival on the absence of change, will especially attract those who have made the greatest profit from change. And so with Southampton, where the old guard is increasingly under siege from the not-so-old guard, the out-and-out *nouveaux* and the funny-money people from both continents.

I go on about Southampton in this mildly obsessive way partly because it represents the last refuge of the ancient social regime whose morals and manners I have always supported against the drug-and-celebrity circus replacing it – only to find one day that I, too, had become part of that circus – and further, because the perfect tranquillity of Southampton now seems a little eerie, arousing superstitions in me which were supposed to have died out with my ancient Greek ancestors: I've grown wary of nemesis in exalted places. For it was from this sanctuary of privilege that, within forty-eight hours in the summer of 1984, my life chose to take a sudden dive to the lowest of the lower depths. That is to say, one day I was playing tennis and cuddling my children in sunny surroundings, the next day I found myself under arrest on drug charges at London's Heathrow Airport.

The exact sequence of that comedy of horrors and my subsequent stay in one of Her Majesty's institutions are the subject of this book, comprised chiefly of the diary I kept in prison. It was not the easiest thing to do, since keeping a diary was against prison rules, but it wasn't the hardest either. Much harder was the life itself and, later, the aftermath of prison – by which I don't mean the loss of face or reputation. These days, alas, going to jail produces a slightly more beneficial effect on one's reputation than, say, receiving a knighthood. Still, I do not like knowing that I'm an ex-con or the prospect of my children knowing it. As for what others think, the stigma that one carries around, such as it is, constitutes part of the punishment and must be endured. I am not an advocate of easy sympathy for criminals and convicts. Not only do I not subscribe to the victim-of-society theory, but having seen criminals and convicts at close quarters I can tell you that they are, almost without exception, selfish, dangerous and untrustworthy.

But I do believe in forgiveness and loyalty from friends and, as always in such situations, you do find out who your true friends are. In general, I discovered that the liberals of my acquaintance were the most hypocritically unforgiving, especially considering the fact that most of them had spent their jolly, drug-addled youth hacking away at the social fabric. But that, of course, was in the service of revolution and therefore acceptable. My conservative friends, speaking both professionally and personally – at the *Spectator*, the *American Spectator*, around Bill Buckley and his circle in the United States, and many others on both continents – proved in contrast to be extremely loyal. I shall be dropping various of their names as they appear in the story.

Above all, however, life in prison teaches you one lesson more than any other: that you are alone, fundamentally and finally alone, and you'd better be self-sufficient. Now, although this insight, too, served as a fortifier in the face of upheavals to come, as a cure it was considerably more depressing than the disease. Sooner or later one gets over disappointment, betrayal, loss. Not so with prison. It doesn't go away. It doesn't change colour or character. Instead, everything else dissolves and rearranges to accommodate this central event. One's past begins to look different. One begins to see oneself in a new and strange light. It is a very particular feeling, and difficult to explain, except to say that you are left with the knowledge that nothing will be the same again. I have often caught myself thinking that my life up to now had been a long and exhilarating dream, from which I had suddenly and irreversibly woken up. That last day in Southampton seems to have been a final snooze. It marked the end of a charmed cycle in my adult life which began – as I morbidly imagine – three decades ago in the same place.

I first visited Southampton during the late fifties. A friend of my parents, namely Basil Goulandris, a millionaire and philanthropist of the Greek ship-owning fraternity, had a house there and we spent a weekend as his guests. I thought the town incredibly pretty, but the life rather on the quiet side. What else I'd expected from a place founded in the seventeenth century I can't imagine. I also remember thinking remotely that this might one day be an idyllic spot to settle down in, with a wife and children. Back then, however, marriage, children and the proverbial white picket fence seemed as improbable as, say, the marriage of Amy Carter to the Ayatollah Khomeini's son.

At that time, my natural habitat was the French Riviera, the once fabled land placed on the discerning sybarite's map by people like the Fitzgeralds, Picasso and Somerset Maugham. In 1958 the Côte d'Azur was still an enchanted spot, especially to a young man finally free of boarding-school after ten years, with enough money and plenty of time on his hands. I did not choose the Riviera at random. Ever since my freshman year at prep school I had dreamed of living in France. While my schoolmates studied hard and prepared for college, I concentrated on learning *Tender Is the Night* and *A Moveable Feast* by heart. As soon as school was over, I headed for Paris, the South of France and the Alps, in hot pursuit of Dick Diver and Papa Hemingway.

Throughout my school days I had worked hard preparing myself for the future. I had learned to box and wrestle;

I was an accomplished tennis player and, while at the University of Virginia, had even learned the rudiments of polo. I also knew how to ski, thanks to the years I had spent at the Salisbury School in Connecticut. (That came after I was expelled from Lawrenceville for conduct becoming a playboy, and before Blair Academy. Still, the skiing was sure to come in handy later on.)

Thus I hit French ground running.

Because of a fortunate accident of birth I was able to enter the most important tennis tournaments of the time. Greece, which I represented, was not exactly a tennis power. The whole country boasted about twenty courts, three of which were private, fifty or so ball boys and ten players, give or take a couple. Needless to say, I was ranked in the top ten. In fact, I was number two for a time.

Paris was even more fun than I had imagined. Under de Gaulle, the French had begun to feel like the Frenchmen of old, something they hadn't experienced for a long time, especially after the defeats of the Second World War, the loss of Indo-China and the débâcle in Algeria. The effect was exhilarating, even on us foreigners. I shared a flat near the Bois with two Argentine polo players. Our mentor and guide was Porfirio Rubirosa, a modern Robin Hood, a Dominican playboy who married rich Americans like Doris Duke and Barbara Hutton and spent their money on himself and his poorer friends, namely us.

I settled into a routine almost immediately. We would get up early, work the ponies and then head for the Racing Club to practise tennis. After a poolside lunch at the club, there would be more tennis, and in the evening we would get together, dine, go to a party and then head for New Jimmy's on the Boulevard Montparnasse, Régine's first great nightclub. After 4 a.m. we would race back to the

Right Bank, to an after-hours jazz place on Rue François
Ier. It might sound like an empty life, which it was, but
even today I can't think of anything better than to be
young and hedonistic and to have Paris as a playpen. As
Papa said, it is a necessary part of a man's education.

After the French championships and Wimbledon, there
would be a bit of polo in Paris, then my friends and I
would pack up and head for the Riviera. The first couple
of weeks would be spent in St Tropez, in those days a
dreamy little fishing harbour unknown to tourists, still
cheap and friendly. Cannes, with the rococo Carlton Hotel,
would be our next stop, followed by the Hôtel du Cap, in
Cap d'Antibes, for the duration. The Hôtel du Cap, you
will recall, was the setting for *Tender Is the Night*, for
the meeting between Dick Diver and Rosemary Hoyt.
Nothing much has changed since Fitzgerald's day except
the personnel.

Just as Fitzgerald's rich spread across Europe after the
First World War – inventing their new summer season
down in Antibes – so the Françoise Sagan crowd spread
across France following the Second World War. The object
was to have fun, as much fun as possible, and to ask
questions later. We all suspected there was a price to be
paid – also later. So much later that not a single moment
of sleep was lost worrying about exactly when and what
that payment would be. The focus of social life on the
Riviera was La Leopolda, the great house in Villefranche
named after the Belgian King Leopold and owned by
Gianni Agnelli. Gianni had his boats racing up and down
the coastline non-stop, ferrying people back and forth to
an endless round of parties, or so it seems now. When
autumn came, the crowd would drift towards the Eastern
Mediterranean and the Greek Islands. From there it would
be New York City and more of the same.

What strikes me now, whenever I look back, is not how relentlessly privileged life was in those years but how I never once questioned the privilege, or the time wasted in exercising it. Tennis and skiing and polo were to me 'all in all', as Wordsworth says of nature. But, unlike his, the days of my youth were not 'bound each to each by natural piety'. Wine, women and sport were nearer the mark, in a life then still governed by good taste, not yet the stuff of vulgar television serials.

In the winter of 1962, in Gstaad – where a three-month stay was *de rigueur* – I met a young woman whom *Paris Match* magazine had named the prettiest débutante of the year. She was Cristina de Caraman, daughter of a French duke and famous for her public rows in nightclubs. Not only was Cristina one of the loveliest girls I had ever met, she had an added attraction: no one, not even a gossip columnist, had ever accused her of being an intellectual. We hit it off like the proverbial terrorist and hand grenade. Soon after, we decided to get married. Marriage is supposed to change a man, to make him more serious towards life, more responsible. I found this conventional wisdom untrue. The only change I noticed was the money saved on taxi fares at night. We continued to live the same kind of life as before – Antibes, Athens, Mykonos, New York, Gstaad, Paris . . . It was a gaudy dream of freedom and fun, but soon the inner fissures of such a life became apparent. I was getting bored with the emptiness, the constant rounds of drinking, the hangers-on, the financial anxiety which goes hand in hand with flamboyant living, the despair of the morning after.

Worse, the tennis had also gone to pot. (Metaphorically that is, because back then the word 'drugs' meant something in neon lights over a Whelan's sign.) Years of sleepless nights had taken their toll. An already weak game was turning into an embarrassing one. After a particularly bad loss to a kid so young he could hardly reach over the net to shake hands after the match, the circuit and I parted company. My skiing, too, was suffering. One needs strong legs to hold the tuck position in the downhill, and when in 1962 – in the Chamonix world championships – I managed to beat only four racers, two of whom turned out to be carpet salesmen from Beirut, that ambition also went down the chute. Polo, however, was still fun and the trophies kept coming, for two obvious reasons: first, the horse does all the running, and second, and more important, polo is a game played by four to a side in which two are professionals who gallop like mad up and down the field while the other two amateurs simply canter gently and elegantly in front of the stand in which the prettiest girls are seated.

So polo it was for a while, but even I realized before long that having polo as a *raison d'être* was commensurate with having the Aga Khan as an idol. Simply ludicrous. I soon gave it up, just about the time, in fact, that Cristina let me know I was impossible to live with. Henceforth, she would continue her party rounds on her own. I wished her luck and we parted friends, whereupon I headed for Athens to the healing bosom of the family. There it was, 1968, ten years after the trip had begun, and I was thirty years of age, unemployed, unmarried, childless and looking forward to a future not even Babs Hutton would envy it promised to be so empty.

Like everything else in this ghastly modern world of ours, Athens is no longer what it was, a beautiful city of half a million souls, with wide, tree-lined boulevards, neo-classical architecture, splendid green parks, a happy populace and the smell of jasmine everywhere. I had spent the years of the Second World War there, and had witnessed things that cannot be considered salubrious for the young.

Nevertheless, by 1968 the war years were long past and I settled down in the family seat trying to figure out what to do with myself. I only knew that I would never go to work in the family shipping business or in the family textile factory. I have always felt that working for one's old man is a bit like wearing 'received decorations', in the manner that royals do. (I once said this to an ex-monarch who to my horror began screaming aloud that I had insulted his family honour. I managed to quieten him down only by offering my brand new Lotus car for a week.)

While contemplating my future in the Hilton Hotel bar one night, I ran into an extremely suntanned man in his early forties who looked familiar. Upon closer inspection he turned out to be *Newsweek* magazine's chief foreign correspondent, Arnaud de Borchgrave, now the editor-in-chief of the *Washington Times*. Arnaud, a Belgian-born count, had covered more wars than Gaddafi has caused. After a few drinks, Arnaud suggested I do something with my life. 'Journalism,' proposed the diminutive count.

A brilliant idea, I thought, with only a slight problem. I had never even written a letter, no less an article, and starting from scratch at thirty in a profession that requires knowledge, discipline and sometimes a small amount of intellect was as daunting an idea to me as trying to row across the Pacific on a Hollywood casting couch. Countering my misgivings, Arnaud improved on his idea. 'Okay, then. Try photojournalism. You can follow me around and learn the ropes.'

Which I did.

I bought all sorts of equipment, took a few lessons from a paparazzo I had often met outside the chic nightclubs of the time, and off I went in pursuit of Capa-like glory. Although I did get some pictures published in *Newsweek* and *Paris Match*, I also realized in no time

that Cartier-Bresson I wasn't. Sitting in hotel rooms at
night while Arnaud interviewed the high and mighty of
this world, I began to practise writing political tracts in
Greek. Two years later I finally got a job as correspondent with an Athenian daily, and one with *National
Review*, Bill Buckley's magazine and Ronald Reagan's
favourite read. From then on, things grew easier. I covered
the Jordanian war of 1970, the Indo-Pakistan war of
'71 – plus the fall of the Colonels in '74 in Athens, the
birthplace of selective democracy.

My writing, to say the least, was distinctly uneven, but
reporting from places like Hue in South Vietnam in 1972
had its advantages. However green one was, the stories
were so big that even someone who wrote television commercials for a living could sound like Tolstoy. War may be
horrible and inhuman, but it makes bad writers write well,
good writers write poetry and unknown writers known.
Under such conditions I wrote adequately, and soon after
the fall of the Colonels an English publisher approached
me about doing a book on recent Greek history. I agreed
with alacrity, and began acting like the reincarnation of
Thucydides in no time.

In the meantime I had also begun to see, on a more-or-
less permanent basis, a beautiful young woman named
Alexandra Schoenburg. Her father was an Austrian prince,
scion of an old family whose members, to their credit,
had been decimated on the Russian front, where Hitler
sent the nobles who were politically unreliable. On 30
November 1975, in New York, my little girl was born.

Having just finished the book, I was looking around for
a job outside Greece, by then the most anti-American
country west of the Soviet Union. Alexandra wanted to live
in Paris, where she had partly grown up, but I preferred
London because of work opportunities. So we stayed

unmarried and mostly apart, and I flew to Paris every chance I had to visit her and the baby. Then a lucky thing happened. I was in a bit of trouble, having written an article charging that some Greek newspapers were on the take from the Soviet Union – a fact confirmed by the *New York Times* man there eight years later. Naturally, one of the culprits I had accused decided to sue me. A kangaroo court further decided to give me sixteen months in the pokey, so one fine day I left Greece – on my yacht, I may add – and headed for places more civilized than the birthplace of tyranny.

In London I was offered a weekly column in the *Spectator*. My subject was to be the rich, the aristocratic, the glamorous and the fashionable of the world, most of whom I regarded with scorn. The column was – and still is – largely a long lament about how awful modern life has become: the tired outrageousness of the rock-and-roll culture, the lurid horror of punkish anarchism, the expensive selfishness of the cocaine world. Writing needed little research, as I drew mostly on my background, but I did revert to my old habits more and more while pretending – especially to myself – that I did so for my work.

By 1980 Alexandra and I had moved to New York together, where I embarked on a similar column for *Esquire*. She was once again pregnant and I had taken my first sniff of cocaine. When my little boy was born I bought a house in the city and another in Southampton, married Alexandra and took my second, third, fourth and fifth sniff of you-know-what. Mind you, I was not a natural doper. I took the stuff only when drunk, never more than twice a week and never during the day. But I took it, and hanging around the nightclubs of the eighties didn't exactly discourage me.

Still, my life was happy. Probably for the first time ever

I was quite content, with fewer demons chasing me and lots of work to take my mind off the ageing process, which was coming on like gangbusters. I had begun to play tennis again, continued to practise the sport I have always loved most, karate, and travelled mostly in order to compete in various karate tournaments. By the summer of 1984, then, life was yielding its sweetest harvest. The children were old enough to be a delight, my house in Southampton was filled with friends every weekend and the career was better than ever. The *American Spectator*, the conservative political monthly, had offered me a column called 'Politique Internationale'.

Then 23 July, a day I shall not soon forget, dawned bright and hot. Planning to fly to London that night, I spent all day on the tennis court, getting nice and tired for the ride. About ten guests were visiting and we had a long softball game on the lawn which we play every year so that my daughter can show how competitive she is. Then, after a late and very liquid lunch, Alexandra and an English couple drove me to the airport.

A week later, Alexandra would meet me. From London, we were to go to Italy to stay with friends; from there, on to Greece to my boat. Needless to say, it was not to be. I had left my passport in my city house. That meant I had to miss my flight and drive into the city instead to fetch the passport.

Leaving me with a free night.

So I headed for a disco.

Now, I have often written long diatribes against drugs in the past, but if anything will make one resort to them, discothèques will. They are loud, full of ghastly people, and spending any amount of time inside them without *some* help is akin to having an arm amputated without ether. So I went to the barman, whom I vaguely knew, and asked if he had anything. 'I've got the best there is,' he answered, 'but you've got to buy the whole thing or nothing at all.' I was not surprised. People who sell drugs are hardly sensitive souls. In fact, they're a loathsome bunch with the integrity of hyenas and the morality of rats. But no one pushed me to buy. I fished out my wad, paid $1800 for twenty grams of coke, stuffed it into my back pocket and headed for the bathroom.

I still think back often and wonder: had I taken any of it that night, would matters have turned out differently? But I didn't. The bathroom was a scene out of Dante so I fled the whole place and went home to sleep. In the morning I went for a run, did some karate with my *sensei*, got my papers together and caught an early flight to London, congratulating myself on not having got wrecked the night before.

The flight was perfect. I had a sound sleep and, upon arrival, was the first one out of the plane and through passport control, with no luggage except a small carry-on. The rest of my clothes were in my London flat. Passing through customs I was asked if I had anything to declare. I said I had nothing. The officer looked through my small bag and waved me on. Then, as I was leaving, I heard a voice say, 'You're going to lose that envelope.'

'Oh, thank you,' I replied, being Taki, 'if only you knew what was in it.'

The man crooked his finger. 'Come back here,' he said.

And that was it.

The first thought that crossed my mind as I entered the cell was that life would never again be the same. The word 'never' has a permanence I've always found hard to digest. On this occasion, however, I remember distinctly that I had absolutely no doubt that some terrible dark shadow had caught up with me for good. Yet, being under arrest is no big deal. I had once spent time in a Palestinian guerrilla jail somewhere in Jordan, and I had been held for two days by the Greek military police. Both arrests, however, were experiences that made me proud. They involved no shame or dishonour, certainly no feeling of humiliation. This, of course, was different. Not being someone who feels that possessing wealth or enjoying privilege is automatically wrong or guiltworthy, I had always refused to regard my hectic pursuit of adventure as necessarily venal. But now I had become one among many whose money and privileges had led them from self-indulgence to self-destructiveness to criminal misconduct.

The cell was located somewhere in the bowels of Heathrow Airport. As I waited for a body search, another thought flashed over me: my morbid fascination with danger was over. After a complete search, the officers read me my rights and the grilling began in earnest. It went on for ten hours. While it was still continuing, late in the afternoon, two agents drove into London and took apart my flat. They found nothing, and upon their return the atmosphere relaxed, the questioning became softer, less hostile. In fact, I was even offered a cup of tea. (I later found out that one of the officers who had searched my flat was a regular reader of my column.)

The grilling is just like the movies. One officer acts like Mr Nice and the other threatens. Both my interrogators wanted to know who else I had taken cocaine with. That, I flatly refused to tell them. I did, however, tell them everything else: how many times I had bought it, if I had ever taken it across national boundaries, the amount I usually bought. I even gave them the name of the club where I had bought the stuff, but used a false name for the barman – in truth, I didn't know his real one. They repeated their early question a number of times: Who else had I taken cocaine with? There was no way I could or would answer. People who took coke were committing a victimless crime, and those who had taken it with me had done so in confidence. So, eventually, when the officers made their final offer, 'Give us a couple of names and then you can go to the bathroom,' I blurted out, for a joke, 'Prince Charles and Prince Andrew.' For a second they looked incredulous, and then they began to laugh. Soon after that we packed it up and headed for a police station, and a real prison cell.

Once there I was booked, fingerprinted and locked up for the night in a windowless cell. Needless to say, one does not sleep in prison on the first night. One paces up and down, and at times sideways, one counts the squares that make up the soundproof walls, plays games in which one wakes up suddenly and finds out it's been a bad dream. Time, however, goes slowly. In fact, one feels like a passenger on an empty platform waiting for an urgent train that refuses to come. Every once in a while, someone clicks open the judas spyhole and checks that the inmate isn't attempting suicide.

As everything had been taken away from me I could tell time only by the activity I could hear outside. Finally, the door was banged open and someone told me to follow an officer. I did. We drove in a Black Maria for about half an hour and then, once again, I was put into a tiny cell and instructed to wait. About three hours later, an officer stopped by and asked me if I had a lawyer. I said no, and was assigned one by the court. Eventually he came in and I told him everything. I also asked him to make sure that no newspapers got hold of the story. He seemed like a nice man who knew his way around, and my spirits rose. But when I was ushered into a courtroom above the cells my heart sank. The whole press gallery was full; I could see some familiar faces among them.

I pleaded guilty to the charge of importing twenty grams of cocaine and then the officer who had busted me, a Mr Richardson, took over. Richardson was the Mr Bad Guy of the previous day. But he must have had either the most pleasant of dreams that night or a terrific bowel movement that morning, or both, because he turned out, now, to be all sweetness and light. He said he was convinced I was carrying the stuff for my personal use, that I had been cooperative and truthful, and for good measure he told the court how I had pretty much given myself away by volunteering the contents in the envelope even before any question of a search arose.

From the corner of my eye I noticed a couple of hacks sniggering. Then my lawyer got up and in two seconds flat I knew my next destination was definitely going to be indoors. Although I had instructed him not to mention that I was a writer, the presence of a small company of Fleet Street hacks made my request redundant. So he banged on about what an important journalist I was, how the pressure of my work had driven me to cocaine, and then, for good measure, he threw in the fact that I was almost as rich as the Queen herself. And, he went on to add, 'In the group he runs around with, cocaine is considered a lesser evil than a good glass of red wine.'

After that remark, of course, louder sniggering came from the press section. But the magistrate, who looked like a kind old boy, and the two ladies who made up the troika deciding my fate, neither approved nor were amused. Before they had a chance to say anything, I raised my hand and asked to be recognized. I was given a minute to confer with my lawyer. 'He now tells me that cocaine is not as widely used as wine in his circle,' was the way my counsellor put it when we resumed. More sniggering and a warning from the bench followed that pearl of wisdom. Finally, the three magistrates retired and I sat waiting while every pair of eyes in the room took in my unkempt appearance, which became more unkempt by the minute as I began to sweat profusely.

When they returned the old boy said, 'The importing of cocaine into Britain is a serious offence. Although the defendant is of previous good character, and the court is convinced the cocaine was meant for his personal use, I nevertheless sentence you to four months in prison.'

I was then taken back into the cells while my attorney appealed, and I posted bail pending that appeal. By mid-afternoon I was free, and I drove into London, five pounds thinner and five thousand pounds poorer. The English summer was just beginning, but to me it felt like the last days of autumn – gloomy, depressing and fraught with a sense of foreboding.

Too embarrassed to return to the old life I fled to the country, to deepest Wiltshire, and remained there for the duration. As I didn't feel like travelling and facing the old man, I even sold my boat – to a Turk, of all people – and she now sails proudly up and down the Bosporus. I took a different lawyer and volunteered to have spot drug tests made in order to show, when my appeal came up, that I was being a good boy and a reformed character. My wife and children came over, but the climate between us was icy. Alexandra simply could not stomach the fact that I had done what I had. She thought, and rightly so, that I had compromised the future of my children, something that made me feel even worse than I already did. My appeal was scheduled for 14 December. I tried to envisage what prison would be like, but I still couldn't believe that I would actually end up there, serving time. All my life I had gone to the brink, yet had somehow escaped disaster. It is unwise to become too dependent on the last-minute intercessions of Lady Luck.

On the eve of my appeal the *Spectator* gave a dinner for me. It was a jolly occasion. Alexander Chancellor, the brilliant ex-editor who had first hired me, gave a speech, followed by Charles Moore, his successor to the job. Jeffrey Bernard, who writes the column 'Low Life' below my 'High Life', and who is also considered the best and funniest writer in Britain, got up very drunk (he is a self-admitted alcoholic), sat down and proceeded to tell a long joke about a man going down on a woman reading George Eliot's *The Mill on the Floss*. And, though no one understood what that had to do with my predicament, we roared with laughter and went on for a nightcap to Annabel's, London's foremost watering-hole.

The next evening there was yet another goodbye party, given by John Aspinall, England's greatest gambler and poshest party-giver, in his club the Aspinall-Curzon. Married to Sally Curzon, Aspinall is an English swell, a sort of Elizabethan aristocrat. Fearless, indomitable and deeply civilized, he loves to be surrounded by fierce, wild animals and people of spirit. On the night of the party in my honour, he filled his fabled club with my poshest friends and there were speeches galore. The English aristocracy loves nothing more than to get up and crack jokes about the imminent demise of one of their friends. I got very drunk and later, at Annabel's, suddenly realized that I was acting silly. Alexandra, too, was upset at the circus-like atmosphere gripping my friends and me. I said my goodbyes quickly and took her home.

Unable to sleep, I wrote my last column, shaved, showered and had a barber come at seven in the morning to give me an old-fashioned crew cut. At eight, a driver took me to South London, to Southwark Crown Court, where Judge Trapnell would be hearing my appeal. Meantime, the children were sent off to America with the explanation that their father was about to leave for Australia – as indeed he would have had to, a century ago – to do research for a book about prisons. As they left I suddenly felt afraid that I might break down. But I didn't, I held up and, to my surprise, found myself telling jokes, even managing to make them shriek with laughter, the way children sometimes do. Separating from them, I wondered what other men go through, how they behave with their families in the last moments before departing for a long prison sentence.

For someone who has always been an unshrinking supporter of law and order, I was already wavering on the question of prison and its benefits. The car sped through the still inanimate streets, and, with London rolling by, I noticed that for the first time in my life I had taken no money with me. I felt a strange satisfaction. The relentlessly privileged life was about to end and a great curiosity, mine, was beginning.

As I walked into court, a light rain had begun to fall.

· 14 December 1984 ·

There's a small catch to taking a case to the Court of Appeal. If the appeal fails, the judge has the right to increase the sentence. Doesn't happen too often, mind you, but the possibility is there, and like an ingrown toenail I became uncomfortably aware of it throughout the months of waiting.

Finally, the day of judgement. Judge Trapnell, resplendent in wig and gown, is flanked on either side by a lady judge. A bad sign, I think to myself.

The first case is that of a large black man, pleasant looking, who was caught trying to smuggle five kilos of hash into the United Kingdom. He is from Ghana. Trapnell throws the book at him. Then it's my turn. My Karamazov-sized hangover evaporates as I step up to the dock. While various clerks shuffle papers and confer with barristers I keep my eyes lowered. I couldn't have raised them to save my life, I feel so embarrassed. Perhaps not in the class of a child-molester, but worse than tax-evader for sure. Sitting in the dock awaiting sentence as a common criminal, accused of a non-political crime at that, will unman the stoutest heart.

To be sure, I found it a great consolation that the staff of the *Spectator* were there *en masse*, some even signalling their support with smiles and waves.

The *Spectator* is the oldest political weekly in the English-speaking world, having enjoyed uninterrupted publication since 1828, the year Schubert died and Tolstoy was born. People like Graham Greene have declared it the best 'read' in Britain. Although I agree with little that Mr Greene utters these days, especially about America, I certainly say 'amen' to his view of this anarchic, mocking and right-wingish weekly, my employer since 1977. Set in a large and pleasant Georgian house in Bloomsbury, the *Spectator* is staffed mostly by Old Etonians. Its annual party and bi-weekly lunches are the stuff of legend, attended not only by the most influential people in politics, academia and the literary scene, but also by bookies, saloon keepers and the odd lady wrestler.

Above all, the *Spectator* is celebrated for its writers. And for its continuing ability to attract the best and most entertaining, simply because it allows its writers to write with the freedom impossible to find anywhere else. Well-known novelists and biographers like Peter Ackroyd, A. N. Wilson and Auberon Waugh are all regular columnists; editors have been known to leave the magazine only to become ministers in Tory governments. And indeed vice versa, Iain Macleod in 1963 being a celebrated instance. This is not to say that the *Spectator* has ever toed a party line. Far from it. What it has always held is an extremely idiosyncratic view, and those who write for it share that view, a view of the world which can only be described as 'reactionary anarchic'.

Working for the *Spectator* has been one of the great pleasures of my life. Each week, I write one thousand words based on my ongoing adventures as a playboy among the *nouveaux riches*, the radical chic and the social mountaineers who have invaded the world's best resorts, hotels and restaurants. I also have *carte blanche* to expose the humbug of politicians and of the very powerful. In eight years I have been sued four times, but the editor has killed only one column.

The only telephone call I made immediately after my arrest was to the magazine's editor, Charles Moore, who, typically, was out to lunch. Charles could be the twin of the Iron Duke, when the Duke of Wellington was a young man. He is the youngest *Spectator* editor ever, having taken over England's oldest weekly when he was twenty-seven. An Old Etonian and Cambridge man, he is the quintessential English gentleman, with his wonderful sense of humour and fair play and his tolerance of his writers' shenanigans. Above all, Charles protects his minions whenever powerful people try to silence them, which they do more often than not. (Writing under English libel laws is not any worse than writing, say, anti-fascist tracts under the Duce.)

My telephone call was taken by the girl temporarily manning the switchboard, the assistant literary editor Lady Claire Asquith, a great grand-daughter of the Prime Minister. (Talented assistant literary editors, especially pretty ones like Claire, do not mind manning the switchboard in a pinch – at least, not when working for the *Spectator*. How many at *The New York Times*, I wonder, would stoop to such depths?) When I informed her of my predicament and asked her to tell Charles I was resigning, effective immediately, she simply said, 'Poor you, will you be filing copy from prison?'

A little later, Moore's reaction was equally understated. 'We would be shocked if our religious correspondent was caught with drugs,' he told me, 'but we sort of expected our "High Life" writer to be high at times.'

I had hoped the appeal might pass unnoticed by the media, but a quick glance towards the press box reminded me that the English public likes nothing more than to read about the public disgrace of a playboy. (Which is how the gutter press in England always refers to me, although I have been quite hard-working for the last fifteen years. In the United States, oddly enough, it's the other way around. Even American hacks refer to me as a writer rather than as an ex-playboy. I write an average of ten columns per month for four different publications. But, as an Italian once said, 'The good men do is oft interred with their bones.' Probably I will always be known as a playboy, which doesn't bother me at all, perhaps because it's true.) At any rate, the press section resembled a Japanese subway train during rush hour.

The prosecution read out the charges in one minute flat. It did not ask for a custodial sentence, adding, for good measure, that the cocaine was for my own personal use. Then John Mathew, Queen's Counsel, began to plead for the defence. QCs are called 'silks' because of the silk gowns they are required to wear. Well, John Mathew's language that day matched his gown. In fact, he laid it on so thick that for a moment I feared the judge might praise rather than condemn me. Mathew spoke for about one hour which, I was told afterwards, was a good sign. Usually, judges ask the defence to get on with it, but on this occasion Trapnell behaved attentively, even nodding his head a couple of times. Mathew argued that here was a man of considerable wealth who could have chosen to live an indulgent life, but had instead become a war correspondent, etc., etc. He pointed out that throughout the late sixties and seventies, and in places like Vietnam and Cambodia, I had never taken drugs, having succumbed to them only lately, owing to my work covering nightclubs in London and New York. At one point he said the word 'overwork', and once again from the corner of my eye I could see the *Spectator* boys smiling sceptically. Mathew summed up by asserting that prison was the last place to send an overworked and sensitive man like myself, that I had already been punished enough, since I was now professionally destroyed. (Well, I had not agreed with him about most things he'd said in my defence – after all, I went to nightclubs for pleasure, never for work – but being 'professionally destroyed' because I lost my *Vanity Fair* column was tantamount to saying that I was friendless because Jerry Zipkin had dropped me from his circle. Indeed, one wit claimed later that losing the *Vanity Fair* column was the best thing that could happen to a writer.)

Judge Trapnell nodded – understandingly, it seemed to me – and my spirits soared. The three judges then rose to ponder my fate.

Ten minutes later came the familiar knock, the bailiff's 'Everybody rise,' and the judges returned. Trapnell fixed me with a look and uttered only two words, 'Appeal dismissed.' Immediately, I was seized by the elbow and led out of the courtroom through a small door next to the dock. As I went, I turned and looked at Alexandra. She seemed confused, not having yet realized that those two words meant I would be a guest of Her Majesty in prison for the next four months. I only had time to wink at her and give her a smile.

Southwark's holding cells, as they are called, are small and clean but windowless and oppressive. Knowing that for the next four months I would be deprived of that most precious of privileges, freedom, did not help matters. The horror of incarceration dawned on me immediately, a combination of claustrophobia and deep depression. It is hard to describe the feeling. I tried to compare my plight with that of American pilots who were kept in cages by the North Vietnamese for years, but that didn't seem to help.

The pilots had landed there while answering their country's call, while I had simply landed myself in this shit through self-indulgence and arrogance.

Self-pity and disgust ruled the day.

As I had nothing to read and no one to talk to, I tried to imagine that I had a pair of chopsticks and was trying to catch flies with them – an exercise practised by the Japanese Budo masters in order to perfect their reactions, as well as their patience. I tried composing poetry, making up aphorisms about prison and inventing new karate techniques. But the time passed slowly.

At six on the dot my door was opened and I was handcuffed to the large black man from Ghana. He smiled sheepishly at my obvious discomfort. Then, along with a half-dozen others, we were led into a prison bus headed for Pentonville, the Dickensian jail that would be my home for the next few months.

Pentonville is one of the filthiest and oldest prisons in England. Built when Queen Victoria was still wetting her knickers, it has remained unchanged ever since. A large jail, shaped like a scorpion, its huge brick walls and barred windows symbolize a repressive Victorian institution where treatment takes second place to security. Pentonville is a short-term prison, thus making it almost a punitive one: the guards know that the inmates will accept anything because of the brevity of their sentence, and therefore tend to take liberties, no pun intended. As we drove through the massive steel door, I took one last look at the outside world. It was dark and depressing. The rain came pouring down. I thought of how there would be no rain falling on me in the near future, and of Verlaine's saturnine poem about the rain falling on one's heart.

Few places inspire so many myths and misconceptions as prison. My English publisher, Tom Stacey, is a prison visitor and had warned me about Pentonville. Unlike Hollywood movies, inmates do not come up to a newcomer and introduce themselves. Those who have done time before know how to get around the waiting part and get processed early. They also know what jobs to go for and what to say, when interviewed, to the screws. That day, most of the people waiting to be processed were recidivists, and a surly lot. And so were the guards doing the processing. I was fingerprinted, then taken into a room where I surrendered everything in my possession except my watch and a small radio with one frequency. After a cold shower, I was issued two pairs of blue jeans, two blue-striped cotton shirts, two pairs of grey socks, one sweater, one denim jacket, one toothbrush, a small mirror, one pair of plastic black shoes, one towel, two blankets, two sheets and one pillowcase. The blankets were soiled and dirty, but the clothes, although old and falling apart, reasonably clean.

Stripped and washed, ritually divested of my outer self, I was uniformed and processed into becoming an inmate like any other. Now there was nothing left to do but to start serving time. I felt something of the muffled panic one experiences as a child on the first day of school, witless and alone, except here humiliation made the apprehension worse. I had yet to exchange a word with an inmate; no one had paid me the slightest attention. When my name was called out, I passed through a large steel door and into a cell block.

Pentonville, with its four long, high and narrow cell blocks, looks like the fingers of a hand. At its palm, so to speak, is a central area with a glass enclosure from which officers bark out commands through a loudspeaker. Each outstretched block has four landings, long galleries of iron railings giving access to innumerable steel doors. The landings are connected by catwalks. Masked wire nets stretch across each landing to prevent people from being thrown down. My cell, number D-31, was mind-numbingly small: 13′ long by 9′ wide by 7′ high. (In Manhattan, people pay $800 a month for an apartment this size but, that's another story.) Some cells sleep as many as four prisoners but, to my relief, only one man was waiting when I entered.

The cell held two steel beds, two wooden desks with two chairs and in the corner two chamber-pots and two plastic pitchers for water. My cellmate looked less than overjoyed to see me as I came in. He grunted something that sounded more digestive than verbal. I assumed that it was a prison custom to play as tough as possible upon meeting a new man. So I made no effort whatsoever towards breaking the ice. After a while he went to sleep, still without saying anything, so I got partially undressed, made my bed and got in. Then I tried to close off my mind and go to sleep. Needless to say, it was impossible. I could smell other men's smells on my blanket. I could hear people talking through their windows – mostly obscenities with racial overtones, all in harsh, bragging sounds. High above, near the roof of the cell, was a window with thick bars stretched across it. I could see a little bit of black sky. So I spent the night mournfully gazing out at the odd star which fast-moving clouds allowed me occasionally to glimpse. It had been an endless day, but the night promised to be even longer.

What was ahead seemed fathomless.

· *15 December 1984* ·

After tossing and turning – and listening to the rending snores of my cellmate – for an interminable night, the longest of my life, I finally drift off to a joyless sleep, just at daybreak, a dawn I can scarcely perceive. I have a strange dream. Somewhere in England I am about to play cricket. President Reagan, seated high on a hill, is watching the match. I am planning to gravitate over to him during the play and ask him for a pardon, but just as my side takes the field and I am about to carry out my intention, a loud knock on the door wakes me up. It is 6.45 a.m. And the realization comes. 'Oh God, I really am in prison.'

My first day as Her Majesty's guest is beginning.

I hear warders banging on the steel doors with their heavy keys and jiggling the judas holes as they inspect waking men inside their cells. Yesterday I was warned that if I didn't get up and about in a jiffy, the door would remain locked at breakfast time. A loud racket erupts just as I arise. Inmates are screaming obscenities, or singing or banging on the walls with plastic cups. I have fifteen minutes to make my bed, wash and shave in my plastic bucket and get dressed before being allowed out for what seems the most gruesome part of the prison day: slop-out!

As I soon discover, there are two urinals that serve over one hundred men – by my estimate, which I'll double-check soon – on each landing. No toilet facilities inside the cells;

one uses chamber-pots which are 'slopped out' each morning. (Someone told me today that angry or depressed inmates have been known to empty their pots over other prisoners who have displeased them.) Next to the urinals are two large basins with a tap over each, and that is where one brushes one's teeth, cleans one's potty and refills one's bucket with water.

As we wait to be let out for slop-out, my cellmate finally speaks. His name is John, he tells me. He is in for violent assault on a policeman. Not a sociable type. While he shaves I make my bed, and vice versa. Once the beds are made and we are both shaved and dressed, we wait for a screw to open the doors so we can join the slop-out rush. And 'rush' is an understatement. But since I ate or drank nothing the previous day I have very little to empty out, so I only take my bucket and fill it with water. Brushing my teeth, however, is a punishing experience. As the basins are located next to the urinals, I have to brush while others slop out, which for all the world is like dining in a public toilet during a diarrhoea epidemic. First, I wonder whether I can go for four months without brushing my teeth. Then I wonder whether human nature will prove so adaptable that I will one day become immune to others slopping out while I brush.

After that vile initiation to prison hygiene, I am locked up once again while men from various wings and landings go down for the first meal of the day. Pentonville has no central dining area. All meals are taken in one's cell. Like most people unfamiliar with prison, except for Hollywood's version, I thought that at mealtimes I would sit with whomever I wished in a vast dining-room, exchanging 'tough guy' talk with men like James Cagney or George Raft. But, again, reality turns out different. My cell is unlocked and, as directed, I go down the narrow iron stairs to the bottom landing where there is a soup kitchen. Talking is prohibited, as is keeping hands in one's pockets. I take with me one plastic knife-fork-and-spoon set, plus one plastic bowl and plastic cup. I chose yellow utensils probably because in such drab surroundings yellow gives one a lift. Then, too, a light colour like yellow also helps one see the dirt, although I am not so sure if that's a benefit.

The breakfast menu consists of four slices of white bread, one piece of margarine, a helping of porridge and a cup of tea. Walking to and from breakfast it is the old-timers, for some reason, who make the most vivid impression on me. They are extremely pale, but they swagger around with the assurance of old boys in prep school. Yet they are hardly an admirable bunch. They swagger, but so do punks on the outside. Strange, how books and movies generally present criminals in a more or less favourable light. Still, from what I've seen so far, books and movies speak with forked tongue.

On the way back to my cell, an old man comes up to me and slips me a brand new chamber-pot. 'Here, this will do for a prince like you,' he says smiling, and showing very few teeth. John tells me that Sid is the orderly of our landing, a professional thief who has spent most of his life in prison. Sid likes it inside, according to John. He feels the screws and the inmates are the only family he has. This is the first act of kindness I've received in what already seems like a year and, ironically, it occurs to me that in terrible situations, such as prison, it might well be precisely those acts that are hardest to handle.

Around 8 a.m. once again we are unlocked to begin work. I thank Sid as he comes around counting the trays. 'We can't have a millionaire like you pissing in an old pot and giving Pentonville a bad name, can we now?' he replies.

He has read about my imminent arrival in the papers; he is thrilled to meet a rich man face to face. (I am thrilled to meet a kindly soul inside.) It is up to Sid to hand out the few utensils allowed in prison – knives, forks, cups and a safety razor once a week. No soap, however, nor toothpaste. They have to be bought with one's earnings, which never exceed two pounds a week, according to my cellmate.

While the rest of the inmates go to work, the newcomers yet again line up for pictures and fingerprints. While we wait I see the same faces I saw last night arriving with me in the van. They seem to be already well-acquainted. They're cracking obscene jokes and telling stories of how they beat the system. A tall, long-haired hippy-looking man spits squarely on the floor. I'm revolted. But none of the other prisoners protests or even seems to notice. Yet I cannot stop myself from looking at the horrible greenish glob, for me the dominating feature in the room. I'm enraged, I want only to attack him, but I do nothing of the sort. Nor do I say a word. Instead, I force my mind to turn to loved ones, to gentler surroundings. Still, the horror of the spit remains. Finally, I move up to be fingerprinted and photographed. Afterwards, we are all marched back to our wing and lined up once again for an interview with a senior officer about jobs.

Mr Wrigley, the senior officer who interviews me, turns out to be a nice man. I list my previous jobs on the outside, as well as the education I've had. He looks up at me and shakes his head. Then he asks what my crime is. When I answer, he shakes his head some more and tells me I'm a fool. 'You're also an embarrassment,' he says. I suggest he assign me to the library, but he shakes his head. 'Do you like *girls*?' he asks. 'Then stay away from there.' In the end he tells me to go back to my cell while he tries

to find me something to do. And, as I leave, to my surprise
he winks at me.

Locked up again, I find myself all choked up. Tears well
up, I'm feeling sorry for myself. And again it's all because
of kindness, this time the kindness shown by Wrigley.
How odd that brutality only makes me tougher. And con-
versely. Why is it, though, that the man who has such
extraordinary power over me can reduce me to tears when
he's kind? I don't know. But it has always been like that.
Is it because I have always felt that my life belongs to
someone else? The old man, my grandfather, the teacher,
etc.? Is it that, since I didn't go out into the big, tough
world on my own, I feel the continual need to thank
another for my existence?

The rest of the day goes extremely slowly. Nothing
happens. I sit in my cell and count the hours. But I'm
starting to feel better. Even faintly optimistic. As far as I
can tell, the worst enemy will be the suffocating routine,
the monotony, although horrors may still be lurking
behind the scenes that I have yet to imagine.

The daily prison schedule goes something like this:

6.30 a.m. – first bell
7.00 a.m. – slop out, shave and dress
7.30 a.m. – breakfast
8.00 a.m. – workshops
11.00 a.m. to 11.45 a.m. – staggered shifts exercise in
  the yard, then back to work
1.00 p.m. – 'dinner'
1.00 p.m. to 2.00 p.m. – lock-up
2.00 p.m. – workshops
4.00 p.m. – 'tea' and then lock-up for the rest of the day

John tells me about the different workshops: laundry,

uniform-stitching, accounting (prison wages), library and gym orderly – according to my cellmate the best job in the whole prison. I find myself believing in Mr Wrigley, believing that he'll come up with the best job of all. It is incomprehensible that a total stranger like Mr Wrigley should already be looking out for me, but that is how it has always been.

The first day of prison is like the first day in boarding-school. At least for me. In both places I began by merely trying to survive in an alien environment . . .

My first day in boarding-school, I found myself in a strange country on my first trip to the Western hemisphere.

It was 1948 when I first arrived at Lawrenceville. I was eleven years old.

Greece had gone through a tough time during the forties. First the Italians invaded in October 1940, and although we beat the hell out of them we suffered enormous casualties. Then in April 1941 Hitler came to the aid of Mussolini, so Greece had to fight both Axis armies. After a bitter occupation, and three years of hunger and depriva-tion, the Communists tried to take over the government by force. In 1948, initially with the help of the British, and then of the Americans, the Greek army was still fighting the Stalin-backed Reds in the mountains of Northern Greece.

My father had fought in Albania against the Italians, and had continued to fight as a member of the under-ground during the Occupation. He published the only pro-Western newspaper in the underground press. My grandfather was Chief Justice of Greece's Supreme Court and, after the Liberation, briefly Prime Minister. Both he and my father were convinced that Stalin would make a move for Greece in the same way he had swallowed countries like Estonia and Latvia, not to mention Poland, Hungary and Romania. So my grandfather and my father decided to send my brother and me out of the country.

Thus we arrived at La Guardia Airport aboard a TWA Constellation in the autumn of 1948, two boys who spoke perfect Greek, German, a bit of French, but not one word of English. Worse, we both wore our finest: plus fours for my brother who was older, and a spanking double-breasted tweed suit for me. Unfortunately, the trousers were knee-length, customary in Greece at the time, and my hair was slicked back with brilliantine, as was also customary among the well-to-do then, in the birthplace of democracy.

Now one can imagine the figure I cut upon arriving at Lawrenceville. I was just as scared as I was coming into Pentonville, but back then I didn't even know the word 'karate' and I had nothing to fall back on. New boys like my brother and me were called 'rhinies'. We had to wear beanies, those peakless caps that American schoolchildren used to have to wear, at all times, except when indoors and while exercising. We also had to stick to the cemented paths that criss-crossed the vast four-hundred-acre campus. Shortcuts by walking on the grass were forbidden.

Obviously it was difficult for an eleven-year-old boy from the Old World to understand the hazing customs and traditions of an old school of the New World. I managed to get so hopelessly lost and confused on the first day that those rather subtle traditions slipped my mind. While running around like the proverbial headless chicken, trying to find where my classes were, all I heard was older boys screaming at me, 'Take a brick, take a brick!'

'Brick-taking' was part of yet another tradition at Lawrenceville. If a rhinie breaks the rules and walks on the grass or fails to wear his beanie, an older boy has the right to make him carry a brick, which the rhinie will then carry everywhere, except, again, when indoors or while exercising. On my second day I had accumulated more than ten bricks and, frankly, had decided to give up. Having spent most of my formative years under an occupier, I did not take kindly to authority, especially one without a uniform and a gun. So I remained in my tiny cubicle, cutting all classes and only showing up for meals in the Lower School dining-room. On the fourth day a master visited me and asked me in very slow English why I was not attending classes.

Being Greek, and therefore a natural actor, I mimicked how badly I had strained my back, then pointed at the large laundry bag containing all the bricks. Then I shrugged my shoulders and began to weep crocodile tears. The result of my little drama was predictable. Dr Healy, the headmaster of the school and a kindly soul, immediately sent down a ukase that forbade any boy younger than thirteen years of age, or weighing less than 110 pounds, to carry more than three bricks. Which, in fact, made it possible for me not to wear the hated beanie and to walk on the grass, as long as I was willing to have three bricks always on my person.

Needless to say, overnight I became known as a troublemaker, as well as a wise guy who beat the system. A lot of older boys began to pick on me, and to pick on me rather hard I might add. It was then that an older boy, Ben Cooper, befriended me and tried to show me the ropes. Ben was a house leader and an all-house football player, but his advice went wasted. One year later I was unceremoniously thrown out for beating up a boy who had virtually tortured me the year before. During my first year I had learned to wrestle and also how to defend myself in a scrap. And hell hath no fury like a twelve-year-old who suddenly realizes his tormentor is a bully and a coward.

My rounds of exclusive prep schools were just beginning.

· *16 December 1984* ·

My cellmate informs me upon rising this morning that of all the days of the week Sundays are by far the worst because we stay locked up for twenty-three hours out of twenty-four. Andrei Sinyavsky, whose moving prison diary I read before coming in, wrote that life in prison is like a moving train. The automatic movement in time creates the illusion that an otherwise empty existence is being filled and made meaningful because, whatever one may be doing, life, and one's sentence, is going forward. I try to think of life and my sentence going forward while I sit on my bed with nothing to read and nothing much to look forward to, and it's hard.

I have already spent most of the night awake, my optimistic mood ebbing away as I realize that the second day in prison is worse than the first. The natural curiosity one has about penal institutions departs as soon as the doors slam shut and the routine is established, which happens almost immediately. You wake up, slop out, you go to work, you have dinner, you go to work, you have tea, you slop out, you go to bed. That's it. You don't look forward to the food or to the work or to the company. All I do look forward to, with the desperation of a dog pining for a bone, are the newspapers and books I hope will be delivered on Monday. English prisons allow inmates to receive newspapers so long as they have been arranged and paid for beforehand. I was so anxious about that that I left nothing to chance. Two weeks before my trial I went around the four main prisons of London and pre-paid the newsagents in the respective locals to deliver the four English dailies and the *International Herald Tribune* to each of the nearby prisons. I trust someone is enjoying them in Brixton, Wormwood Scrubs and Reading jail.

Of course, my cellmate's remarks about Sundays depress me immensely. This is the third time we have spoken. We have nothing to say to each other. I'm sure he cares as little for me as I for him. John spends all his time lying in bed looking at the ceiling. Occasionally he rolls some tobacco. He reads nothing and gives the impression he's happy he doesn't. Today, we each received our one sheet of paper and one envelope, as we shall every Sunday.

For the first time in my life I am truly able to understand what it is to be grateful for small mercies. This morning we have cornflakes for breakfast. We also have an egg which I give to Sid, who immediately gives me some soap in return. So finally I am able to wash my hands with something more than water, as I haven't since leaving home. On Sundays (and on holidays, so Sid tells me), we have an extended exercise period in the yard. God, am I looking forward to it! For all the obvious reasons, of course, but also because, in Hollywood movies, this is where it all happens. Once more, though, the reality leaves me bitterly disappointed. The yard turns out to be just a small space between the four wings, a space about the size of a small backyard tennis court. In it the prisoners walk hopelessly round and round in a clockwise direction.

The Rastafarians, and there are plenty in Pentonville, just stand about in front of the toilets smoking, looking sullen and threatening. The rest walk around at a doleful pace. I try to walk as fast as I can, covering approximately two to three miles in forty-five minutes, by my reckoning. But it is unpleasant work, dodging gangs of men who block the narrow path, spit non-stop and hoot at me scathingly for trying to get some benefit from the exercise period. Although this is my first real contact with the rest of the prison population, I get the feeling that doing anything in a constructive spirit seems to arouse their immediate resentment.

This is so because constructive behaviour often indicates to the criminal mind that you are the sort of softie who subscribes to the notion that one can make something of oneself or improve oneself by application. From my past experience with losers and tough guys – and they're one and the same – they seem to be unwilling to accept responsibility for what they have brought upon themselves. It would mean that they, not the system, not society or fate, have caused their present predicament.

I also discover, while walking round and round looking and listening, that there are no guilty men among us. Everyone has been 'fitted up'. Even the man I was handcuffed to on my way to Pentonville, the nice Ghanaian, said something about how it wasn't his fault he had been caught with a mountain of dope. I guess whining and lying to oneself is part of criminal behaviour, and most criminals are liars and whiners. None of the men I've met up to now seems ever to have heard of that old chestnut, 'If you can't do the time, don't do the crime.'

A young man who also walks briskly, who turns out to be an Irish lad doing a year for stealing, tells me that the exercise period is normally cancelled when it rains – which, of course, it does almost every day. It doesn't today, thank heaven. When I tell him that in New York his lawyer would have plea-bargained him off with a suspended sentence, I think I see a glint in his eye.

Soon I notice four men in the yard with large stripes of bright yellow cloth strapped on to their uniforms. It means they tried to escape. They are not allowed to mix with the rest of us, except in the yard. One of the four looks very old, as if he has given up altogether. Another has a disturbed, scrambled expression on his face – the look of someone just after a major car crash. He belongs in an asylum for the insane, poor fellow, certainly not among criminals, some of whom are making fun of him. The other two look as normal as the rest of us: angry, sullen and caged-up.

After dinner, served on Sunday at 12 noon or earlier, once again we are locked up. I wonder whether to write a letter to Alexandra telling her I'm all right, or to use the paper for my diary. Paper and keeping a diary are forbidden in prison. So far I have been writing in between the lines of a brick-like paperback book, the only book I was permitted to bring. It had to be an instructional volume, so I picked Paul Johnson's *Modern Times*. (Johnson is a colleague from the *Spectator*.) So densely erudite is it that I knew prison would be the one place I could actually devote the time required to read it from cover to cover. Ironically I see that I have described my depressed mood between lines where the author discusses Freudian analysis and the phenomenon of guilt. It suddenly dawns on me that there is another reason why there are no guilty men in prison. Guilt is something only people who are free can enjoy.

After my bust, and throughout the long wait for my sentencing, I felt enormous guilt, especially at what I had put my wife and children through, but the moment I entered jail, guilt was the last thing that entered my mind. I imagine this is self-preservation, since adding guilt to the problems one has to face in everyday prison life would be too much to bear, even for the toughest of men. I don't think the absence of guilt, here, occurs because all prisoners have a warped conscience, allowing them to do the wrong thing without inner turmoil. Many do, but not all. Political dissidents in the Soviet Union and other parts east manage to survive conditions which would kill the rest of us in no time because they know they are innocent, that they've committed no crimes, and they refuse to surrender to injustice. Criminals, on the other hand, deep inside, do know that they have committed crimes and consequently they are much quicker to give up, whine, beg and become stool-pigeons. On the surface, though, they admit nothing and, more often than not, surmise that anyone genuinely trying to rehabilitate himself is a coward.

· *17 December 1984* ·

This morning I turn on the little one-band radio each
prisoner is allowed and listen nostalgically to the traffic
report. It is followed by the news, which informs me that
forty years ago today the Battle of the Bulge had begun.
The next item sends my mood swiftly downhill. Rita Hayworth, it reports, had a daughter with Orson Welles on
this same day in 1944, which brings to mind her other
daughter, by Ali Khan, namely Yasmin Khan, the sister of
my arch-enemy the Aga Khan.

As everyone who reads the gossip pages must know, the
Aga Khan is the spiritual leader of about ten million
Muslims of the Ismaili sect. His followers consider him a
living God, which is fortunate for him since their beliefs
induce them to pay him regularly a percentage of their
income.

The Khans began as small-time hustlers in Iran, collabor-
ated with the British against a local rebellion and ended by
calling themselves descendants of Muhammad. Karim is
the fourth Aga Khan, and one of the world's richest men.
He owns palatial homes in France, Switzerland, Sardinia
and Africa. The quintessential jet-setter, he spends his
summers in Sardinia and his winters in St Moritz, attending every chic European turf meeting and Rothschild ball.
He also owns two of the most expensive private yachts in

the world, and a private jet or two. Karim and I have been feuding for more than twenty-five years. It all began in Gstaad, in 1958; typically, over a girl. Since I do not believe in giving details about ladies, I will say no more, except that Karim is not the type to take defeat graciously.

In 1962, during the world ski championships in Chamonix, France, I managed to make him hate me even more. I was skiing for Greece, and the Aga had made it as a member of the British team, though he was to compete for Iran four years later when he failed to make his old team. (His mother is British, and he carries a couple of passports.) In the slalom and giant slalom, Karim finished higher than I did, but when it came to the downhill, the living God declined to take part. Chamonix is notorious for having one of the world's fastest and most dangerous downhill runs, La Piste Verte. Two racers who fell during training were in serious condition in the hospital. And Karim, a prudent man, was not about to risk demonstrating his mortality. Or so I gathered at the time. When I finished the course, coming in forty-fifth out of eighty, I had the bad taste to give a mini-interview to a local reporter, lamenting the fact that living Gods were so timorous these days.

You can imagine the rest.

The Aga, needless to say, struck back dramatically twenty-two years later. That is, one week ago. Three days before going into Pentonville, I was informed that a writ for libel had arrived at the *Spectator*'s offices. (Eventually I settled out of court, paying him enormous amounts of money for having written that he collects, rather than pays, taxes.)

So, today, listening to the radio about Rita Hayworth

reminds me of all the good times I've had pulling the Aga's leg in the various resorts where he spends his time, among all those beautiful people he takes so seriously, be they ever so mortal. It also reminds me that for the present the Aga must be feeling extremely satisfied. He is, after all, only human. Knowing that a pest like me is languishing behind bars must make even a stiff and boorish fellow like Karim glad to be alive.

On my way to breakfast, a man yells down to me in Greek from another landing, calling me by my name and making a sign that we should speak later, just as the screws grab him and tell him to shut up. Then, while walking in the yard, he approaches and introduces himself as Pavlo. He is a Greek Cypriot, doing six years for drug dealing. He seems an awfully nice fellow, giving me endless advice and invaluable tips on how to beat the system. Most of it, alas, has to do with how to smuggle in drugs. 'You have your wife or girl,' he says, 'put the stuff inside her mouth, and then when she comes in to see you, she kisses you for a long time. Then you slip it inside your bottom, as it's the only place the screws are not allowed to look.' Pavlo is obviously high while he's telling me all this, and when I ask him how he can be high so early on in the day, he answers that the earlier it is, the better. 'The day goes fast when you're high.' He smiles a gentle and sheepish grin.

Once, for the same offence, Pavlo spent six months in a Pakistani jail, in a cell built for six, but which held no fewer than forty-five people. There were no toilet facilities; people just relieved themselves wherever they pleased inside the cell. And once a week they were let out, to clean out the you-know-what.

Pavlo must be a fool to take such chances in places like Pakistan. Or very greedy. He shows me a picture of his wife, and the daughter he's never seen outside the prison visiting room. Abruptly I stop feeling sorry for myself and feel sorry for him.

As I was warned might often happen, the exercise period is cut short when it begins to piss with rain. Once locked up in the cell, however, I find the first pleasant surprise to come my way in the three days I have been inside. Four beautiful newspapers await on my bed, along with a letter from Alexandra, obviously written just after the appeal. Her letter informs me that all major newspapers carried the story of my imprisonment, and that she worried that it would be picked up by the American press, that somebody might leak it to our daughter.

Looking at today's newspapers I am dismayed to see that *Private Eye* carries a fictional account of my first night in jail: how I was miserable and had begged for extra privileges, and how a girlfriend of mine, Lady Cosima Fry, had sat outside Pentonville in the rain waiting to catch a glimpse of me through the bars.

So much for the accuracy of gossip columnists. What is annoying is that Alexandra's feelings are bound to be wounded. Furthermore, it really is humiliating, this idea of my being scared and begging. (That it's a lie outrages me even more, as I did nothing of the sort, although I sure felt like it.) Unfortunately, people tend to believe the shit gossips write, especially the vicious and malicious variety peddled in certain English papers. Unlike Herb Caen or my good friend Liz Smith, both of whom write amusingly and more or less accurately about celebrities, the English gossip columnists are just plain snide.

But, as they say, good things come in pairs, for just as I embark on my first newspaper of the day, the door is unlocked and I am told to report to the gym immediately. The guard escorts me down the landing, past the 'Rule 43'

cells ('Rule 43' means that one is not to come into contact
with the rest of the prison population. The group in these
cells is comprised mainly of child-molesters and stool-
pigeons, or grasses), and on to the gym.

The gym, it appears, is basically a basketball court with
a few trimmings. It is painted brown and has some
contraptions sticking out of the walls on which hang a
boxing-bag, some parallel bars, a badminton net and an
old-fashioned weight-lifting machine. At the end there is a
small office where the instructors have tea, and close by, a
shower room with four showers plus a small compartment
housing sneakers and clean teeshirts and shorts.

Mr Leggett is the senior officer in charge, which means
he wears a white shirt rather than a blue one and sports
two stars on his epaulettes. He runs the gym, and he tells
me he has been a prison officer all his adult life. He is a
short but muscular man, avuncular looking, and he turns
out to be very kind. It just so happens that the previous
gym orderly is being released from prison, and Mr Leggett
has called Mr Wrigley to ask if there is anyone reliable for
the job, truly – as John, my cellmate, mentioned – the best
and most sought after in the slammer. It means one can
shower every day, change clothes twice a week, and it also
means that one doesn't need to work in the steaming
laundry or the bag-stitching assembly line. Above all, it's
an end to all those extra hours stuck inside the cell.

After a brief interview, Mr Leggett informs me that the
job is mine, with one small condition – and here again I
see a glint in his eye – only 'if you can make a good cup of
tea'. I tell him I'm a quick learner.

Ironically, the departing orderly's name is Karim. He's
a large black man with an intimidating build. He shows
me the ropes, literally, for a while, and then suddenly asks
me to fight him. I've no idea how he knows about me, but

all he says is, 'Come on, let's see how tough you are, karate man!' before launching into me. He swings right around in a classical roundhouse back kick, which he fakes, however, before landing a strong back-fist strike on my jaw. I am numb with fear and surprise, but I manage to shake my head clear and hold him off with blocks, until I find an opening and back kick him as hard as I can in the groin. This takes some of the fight out of him, and I go in with a sharp foot sweep that deposits him on his back. Before he jumps up I signal to him that I've had enough, and to call it a day. Mercifully, he agrees. He walks away as if nothing has happened. I go into the shower room to make repairs, where I run into yet another physical education instructor, Mr Heavy, who watched the whole thing but did nothing to stop it.

'Karim is a nice bloke,' he says, 'but he's a bit nuts. Won't be long before he's back inside, I imagine.'

They say the more stupid the dog, the more it barks. Violent people, I have found out, are like stupid dogs. For them violence is the equivalent of barking. One would think that the common plight of being in prison would create an immediate bond. Not in this case, however. Karim wanted nothing of mine, he simply had to fight. He must have known that I did karate from overhearing Mr Wrigley describe me to Mr Leggett. And his reaction was commonplace. Men have always tried to prove themselves, and the shallower they are, the bigger the need. Throughout my karate career I have met many bullies and, unlikely as it sounds, they often do make the grade. In prison, I imagine, there will be those who will want to challenge me, especially if they know that I have not attended the school of hard knocks.

Although I abhor violence, I tend to be a violent person

when provoked. I imagine it comes from a vast insecurity, and perhaps this is why I have never yet fought someone smaller or less tough than myself. But whereas skiing and polo may be a welcome respite from the boredom of living well, a sudden fight with a large black man in prison has taken all the boredom out of my life. I decide to keep an extremely low profile in future.

· *18 December 1984* ·

On my way to breakfast this morning I sense an indefinable restlessness and excitement in the air. Cons are fidgeting and loitering and looking around. I wonder for a moment if they are planning a riot, but then I realize that the screws are far more experienced than I, that they would have noticed if something was up. But they don't seem unusually troubled. It turns out to be nothing more than the arrival of George Best.

George Best had more talent and ability and grace than anyone that's ever played the game of football, but it all went down the drain because Georgie was an Irish lad dogged by the demon that most Irish lads are vulnerable to. That and women, bless his soul. By the age of thirty-eight, having made and blown a fortune, Georgie was broke, debt-ridden, alcoholic and senseless enough to beat up a policeman who had stopped him for drunken driving. The judge gave him three months inside.

He looks bewildered, as everyone does on his first day. This is his first time, too, and watching him I can certainly understand what he's going through. But to give you an idea of what jail does to one, my only concern is whether he might take away my job in the gym. Still, the newspapers have reported that Best will not stay in Pentonville for more than three days. He will then go to an open prison, or a 'country club' as they are called the world over. These are prisons without walls, where white-collar criminals make up ninety-nine per cent of the population. Inmates sleep in dormitories and are allowed to do sports all day. There is no enforced labour and prisoners are free to visit nearby pubs. Unfortunately, drug cases, however small the amount involved, are prohibited by law from being sent to an open prison, as is anyone likely to abscond to another country. Best, of course, is being sent there because of his fame and also because there is a large and successful open-prison football league.

Breakfast is the usual porridge, baked beans and tea. Then it is time for my first day as gym orderly. I'm supposed to hand out sneakers, teeshirts and shorts to those who have not become too cynical to stay in shape. Then there is a certain amount of sweeping up and putting away of things which I've handed out, once each hour is up. Then I repeat the procedure when the next group comes in. This morning we have a basketball game and, since they need an extra man, Mr Heavy asks me to join in. The English simply cannot play the game; it's more like a female wrestling match. Most Englishmen grow up kicking balls to each other; from the waist up, they remain dismally uncoordinated.

I haven't played basketball since I was a boy, back in Greece. In fact the game brought about my first run-in with the law as far back as 1946. I was nine years old and captain of the third grade. Although my school, Makri as it was called, was supposedly the most exclusive in the land, it was not about to supply third graders with uniforms one year after the war had ended, especially while the civil war still raged in the north. We were playing our arch-rivals the fourth grade, and as the newly appointed captain I decided to do something to enhance our morale. I bought uniforms for my team and we actually beat the fourth graders by a score of six to four.

Unfortunately, my dedication to team morale was a little too single-minded. The funds for the uniforms did not come out of my pocket money. Back in 1940, just before my father had departed for the front, he had left some gold coins in his safe and told my mother that if something were to happen to him, if we were to lose the war, she could always survive on the value of the gold sovereigns he had left behind. By 1945 Greece was a ruined country, the currency was totally debased and our factories had been blown up. When my father left for America with a diplomatic passport, he once again issued the same instructions. By then, however, my brother had developed a fascination for all things mechanical and loved to tinker with anything he could dismantle. His favourite game was to play with the combination of the safe. After years of sustained effort, one day in 1946 we suddenly heard a click, the handle turned to the left, and there it was: a small fortune in gold coins. Harry, being unimaginative, stared in amazement and moved hurriedly to shut it, but not before I stuck my hand inside and grabbed a handful. Although he didn't protest too much, he took nothing and said little.

Naturally, I didn't get away with it. The headmaster informed my mother that I had provided the team with uniforms. (Also, in a separate incident, an uncle caught me inside a movie theatre after I had bribed a ticket girl to let me in. The movie, I remember, was called *Kismet*, starring Ronald Colman and Marlene Dietrich. It was wonderful.)

I was in class when the headmaster walked in and asked me to follow him out. As we walked on and right through the school gates, I saw military police. I immediately realized that the rumours we had heard were true. My grandfather had been appointed Prime Minister by the then head of state, Viceroy Damaskinos. (As Chief Justice, Grandpapa was the ideal choice to preside over the period leading up to the first free elections Greece was to have in over ten years.)

As soon as he was informed, he had asked that my brother and I be brought to the ceremony. It took place in the old ochre palace of King Otto, the first Greek king. Soon after the ceremony, however, my grandfather had the head of police, the feared General Evert, interrogate me in his private office. (Like a fool, I fell for the ruse.) I confessed everything, and put all the blame on Harry, who, being the older brother, I felt was duty-bound to take the heat. He hasn't yet forgiven me. Or forgotten.

Attending the swearing-in of Prime Ministers and playing charades with heads of police seems light years away this morning. Perhaps because of karate, or the time I have spent travelling around the world as a journalist or tennis player, I don't feel the great change once in prison. Being on the tennis circuit, especially at the time I was on it, meant flea-bag hotels, cheap restaurants and steerage-class travel. Reporting from Vietnam and Pakistan, not to mention Bangladesh, kept one honest, as they say. Before coming into Pentonville a lot of my friends worried about the food or the lack of comfort. I did not. Living alfresco in Hue in 1972 made sure of that.

My first day in the gym goes rather smoothly. After I clean up, I'm allowed to walk back to my cell unaccompanied, the rest of the inmates having already been locked up fifteen minutes before me. This gives one a sense of superiority I'm told, if only because it offers one of the few opportunities for a prisoner to feel a bit different from the rest.

An odd thing happens after the evening exercise period, which is conducted between three and four in the afternoon. I am approached by a con who tells me he has just swallowed seven morphine tablets, and asks if I want one. I thank him but decline, as I think I've learned my lesson in that regard. Sid offers me two razor blades because he says I'm about to be moved to another cell for reasons unknown. I don't know what this means and whether I should be worried. I take the opportunity to ask Sid what he's in for. 'Stealing,' he replies, and smiles.

• *19 December 1984* •

I turn on the radio this morning and am transfixed by a song I haven't heard for thirty-two years, 'I Saw Mommy Kissing Santa Claus'. It is depressing to think that Christmas is almost here. I know instantly and exactly how many years ago I first heard the song because back then I was doing time in a prep school at Salisbury, Connecticut. I had been thrown out of Lawrenceville just before Thanksgiving of 1952, and my father had convinced Dr Langton, the headmaster of Salisbury School, to give me another chance. Dr Langton was a wonderful man. When my daddy began to describe how I had been traumatized by war and revolution, he just about started to cry. 'Of course he shall have another chance,' said the good headmaster.

He should have said, 'and another, and another, and another'. How well I remember his goodness, his broad, open face, his ruddy complexion and full head of white hair. Straight out of central casting for a pedagogue. Yet my mind flashes sadly back to those halcyon days which at the time seemed as boring as jail is today. Only there was a big difference. Back then, I was certain that one day I would win Wimbledon. I also felt pretty sure that by the end of my life I would be considered one of the civilized world's greatest assets.

Thirty-two years later, optimist though I still am, it is

time to face facts. Not only did I not win a Wimbledon title, I hardly won a round in a major tournament. Worse, far from ending up an important figure on the world's stage, I have become so unimportant that the powers that be have dispensed with my name and I am now reduced to a number. N 72-936, to be exact. There is a tide in the affairs of men which, when taken at the flood, leads on to fortune; but once missed, as the bard didn't say, may catch you in its undertow.

After slop-out Mr Wrigley comes into my cell and says that I am moving to another cell. He offers no explanation. I think it has to do with orderlies – who keep different hours from the rest, albeit by ten minutes at the most – having to live together. My new cellmate in cell D-16 is the same man who tried to pass me some morphine yesterday.

I smell trouble.

Tony the Loon, he calls himself. When we introduce ourselves, he tells me he is doing nine years for a bank job and has about three years to go. He has been brought up from Stafford Hill jail so that he can receive visitors from his family who live in London. He's short, blond, bearded and muscular, with Gene Wilder-like eyes and a swaggering manner. According to him, he's been a criminal all his life. I assume his nickname originates from his crazy look. Tony volunteers the information that he prefers Pentonville because inmates are locked up, unlike his previous lock-up where they're allowed to wander free from cell to cell and only landings are locked. I suppose real criminals like him have a need to feel the discipline of punishment. I try to get him to talk about this particular need, but he clams up. He sees me as an amateur, probably a fool who got caught doing something that had no monetary reward and involved very little danger.

After breakfast he rolls the biggest joint I've ever seen and offers me a drag. I decline politely. Drugs accentuate one's mood, and I'm hardly in the kind of mood that needs intensifying. But Tony makes me nervous. If a screw should happen to barge in, we'll both end up on the 'block' (the punishment cells, where, I'm told, one stays naked without bed or furniture or anything to read). Worse, I will automatically lose days off my remission.

Tony prides himself on being the best getaway driver in London. The only reason he got caught, he explains, was that he was too stoned while pulling a 'job' and skidded off the road with the fuzz right behind him. While he drones on about his exploits, I remember an occasion when I was in the most fantastic high-speed chase. But I don't bother to tell him, realizing that anyone who has been chased for real crimes is hardly going to be impressed by my story.

In fact, it took place only last year. I was in Annabel's, the best nightclub in London, if not the world, and I was with a friend who during the sixties was a formula-one racing driver. Mike Taylor raced during the golden days of British racing. His team-mates at Lotus and BRM were people like Stirling Moss, Jack Brabham and Jimmy Clark. Taylor never won a world championship, but was considered among the best drivers of his time – cool, very fast and somewhat unsafe. He was also a gentleman driver, in for the thrills rather than the money. He retired in the early seventies, one of the few formula-one drivers to do so, so early and still sound of limb.

That particular night at Annabel's he and I got rather drunk, and as we drove away from the club with two girls, we noticed a police panda car following. Now, being caught over the booze limit in England is no laughing matter. With previous offences to consider, as there were in my friend's case, well, the only sensible thing to do was just what he did. He turned a corner, stepped on the gas and rocketed off. So, unfortunately, did the police.

The experience was extraordinarily vivid. At half past three in the morning London's streets are blessedly empty. As roads and buildings raced by I tried to catch a glimpse of the speedometer, but it was hard to focus on it. Taylor was downshifting, double-clutching, braking and accelerating in a manner that made it impossible. We were doing over one hundred miles an hour down Park Lane and while I held my breath, we four-wheel drifted around Hyde Park Corner, barrelled down through the Mall, through Fleet Street and up into Holborn with the cops not losing an inch on us. Mike kept shouting about how good a driver the cop was, while the girls in the back screamed every time we swept around a corner.

Finally, we had covered enough ground to realize that the mad pursuer wasn't going to give up. Taylor also realized that if he let himself get caught now, having broken every law in the book, his prison diaries would be a lot longer than mine. For suddenly he rammed on the handbrake and screeched into a 180-degree turn on the spot. We saw the police car sail past, attempt the same manoeuvre and disappear down a street sideways. At this point my friend's coolness under pressure really displayed itself. He ditched the car. We then hailed a cab and went back to Annabel's, where he immediately called the police and described in irate tones how his BMW had been stolen by some crazy punks.

I have trouble going to sleep again tonight, despite the fact that I deliberately trained very hard in the gym. Tony plays his radio non-stop and talks at an even quicker pace than the DJs. I'm beginning to realize how much I prefer my taciturn ex-roomie.

Three letters arrive. One from a girl I met in Israel while covering the Yom Kippur War. She read in the papers about my conviction, she says, and decided to send her support. Daphna Parag was an Israeli liaison officer based in the Hilton Hotel during October 1973. Every day I would come back from the Golan Heights to file my copy and recount tales of bravery on my part that would have put to shame a story-teller from *A Thousand and One Nights*. Daphna was young and naïve, and extremely patriotic. We had an innocent little flirt that culminated when I had to return to the birthplace of selective democracy. We wrote to each other for a while, but we never saw each other again. Now she has sent the nicest of letters, wondering if I was taking stuff back then when we were together, 'when you were acting so strange at times'.

Well, I certainly was not, never had at the time, and was acting strange because I had to file twice a day, and had to drive up to the front to do it. In other words I was a bit nervous, and the only time people take dope is when they're bored, not when they're nervous. At least, speaking for myself.

Then a message from Tom Stacey, the publisher of my first book and a distinguished writer himself. A prison visitor, and therefore in the know, he sends in lots of advice and good cheer. Educated at Eton and Oxford he was chief foreign correspondent for the *Sunday Times* and won the 'Journalist of the Year' award. His novel, *The Hostile Sun*, garnered numerous prizes and he has written four more since. Tom is one of my closest friends, his letter makes me want to get out and see him. Visit his house, rather, where he's a wonderful host, with his beautiful wife and the best-looking secretaries in the whole of England.

There is also a letter from Lady St Just. She's a White Russian who married Peter Grenfell, or Lord St Just. I've been in love with their two daughters for some time. Katya and Natasha are great beauties, with the kind of looks that can haunt a man, but would not exactly make them candidates for a Hollywood role today. In other words, they possess both mystery and intelligence in their looks, not just a lot of blonde hair and big boobs. Maria St Just is a woman of small physical size with the most extraordinary personality. Tennessee Williams's heroine in *Cat on a Hot Tin Roof*, Maggie, was based on her. (She was the executor of his will.) The sound of her voice inspires awe in the smartest salons of the land – by that, I mean London's most intellectual and aristocratic circles, not what goes for 'smart' in the jet-set. She's a dear, dear friend and, despite my various shenanigans, has always stuck by me. As did her husband Peter, a most wonderful-looking man who, unfortunately, would fall into the deepest depressions when not in the company of various female lovers.

Peter was always extremely polite and kind, but he had a disconcerting habit. He would wake up of a morning, announce that he was going into town to get some cigarettes, and disappear for one or two years. He died recently and Alexandra and I went to his funeral at the family seat in Wiltshire, a grand house and grounds by the name of Wilbury Park – the first Palladian house built in the sceptred isle. (The very same house, in fact, I retreated to while waiting for my appeal.) It was a haunting occasion suffused with lovely autumn sunshine, with someone playing 'Taps' and the whole village trailing in procession to honour their Lord of the Manor. England has abandoned so much of her ceremonial tradition, it was marvellous to see some echoes and shadows of her civilized past still preserved in the countryside.

It occurs to me that, as Christmas looms, all the swells in the land will be returning to their roots in grand country houses. And I will be stuck here, with Tony the Loon and the rest, and Wilbury will at last have its errant master back for good.

· *20 December 1984* ·

Once again I sleep badly, if at all. Tony plays the radio all night, smokes joints non-stop and pops pills. He becomes progressively loud and incoherent, and almost abusive as I keep refusing to join him in his morphine-induced utopia. Earlier on, he told me that he gets his dope from his wife who visits him daily because he has been serving time in the boondocks and is up here only for the Christmas holidays. (The rest of us are allowed one visit every twenty-eight days.) I remember what he has told me about how dope gets through in prison, through a visitor's kiss and then hidden up you-know-where, where authorities are not allowed to look. A strange rule, to say the least, but thinking forward to my visiting day, I thank God that I shall not be subjected to such humiliating procedures. Furthermore, now that I know how dope gets through, I have one more good reason to decline.

I ask Tony what he's been doing for sex the last six years. 'Boys,' he answers. 'I'm no queer, mind you, but we have these male whores that we use.' In return, he says, the whores get protection and tobacco, in that order.

After a night of such company in lieu of sleep, I am in a bad mood at breakfast and I complain about the food for the first time since coming into Pentonville. But my mood improves on my way back up when Mr Wrigley and Mr Holliday, another senior officer, show me a cartoon in the

Evening Standard. It has three screws all dressed up in their parade best, serving three trays full of goodies with a bevy of flunkeys hovering about. The caption reads, 'Sorry, officer, you must go to the executive cells, that's where Mr Taki, Stacy Keach and George Best are staying.'

I have never met Stacy Keach, but one of the reasons I was sure I'd be going to prison was that, one week before my appeal, poor Keach had been sent down for nine months. Probably he got more time than I did because (a) he pleaded not guilty despite having been caught red-handed with the stuff, and (b) because he had hidden it rather ingeniously inside his shaving-cream tube. Although Keach was lucky to be sent to Reading jail, I nevertheless felt very sorry for him. He got a lot of stick from the press and from everyone who happened to read that he had cried on the stand. It was extremely unfair. Keach was not feeling sorry for himself, but rather crying over his stupidity and decadence. Actors and actresses are my least favourite people, but they are an emotional species and they should be allowed to blub a bit during a difficult situation.

Another reason I felt sorry for Stacy was that I was sure his career would suffer disproportionately to his crime. Nowhere are the rules of the river ('Don't get caught!') applied more stringently than in Tinseltown, a place that is not only associated in people's minds with drugs, but one that has glorified them. Perhaps if he were a Hollywood producer who had stolen cheques belonging to others he might have been given a second chance, but an actor is judged on his pulling power, and that has definitely been diminished by his bust. Mr Wrigley had already hinted to me that Keach was having a bad time at Reading because of his 'tough guy' image on screen, as opposed to his sensitive nature in real life. Wrigley said that he was now working in the library after having had a couple of thugs jump him.

After lunch, Mr Heavy takes me outside the wing while I deposit the dirty clothes of the gym in the laundry room. He shows me a wall with hundreds of tiny crosses carved on it. These indicate the number of people who were hanged and buried within the prison walls until their families claimed their bodies. Hangings continued at Pentonville until 1964. The last foreigners to be executed were six German soldiers, POWs who had murdered a fellow German prisoner for refusing to participate in an armed insurrection at the camp where they were being held. This was in the very last month of the war with Germany. The oldest to hang, according to Mr Heavy, was twenty-one years of age. They refused the last cigarette, sang 'Deutschland Über Alles' and died yelling 'Heil Hitler'. They are still buried somewhere underneath a large willow tree in the yard.

Although I have German blood in my veins, and was speaking the language before I knew a word of Greek, I'll be damned if I understand the Germans. They produced Goethe, Schiller, Hölderlin, Beethoven, the greatest tank commanders in history, the noblest warriors and also Eichmann, Mengele and the Baader-Meinhof gang. I remember being in Italy when an acquaintance of mine who had been kidnapped was released. The police were saying that his abductors must have been Germans because he was tortured so brutally in captivity. (He was put inside a pine box and, every time he moved, the razors which lined the inside of the box would cut into him.) Sure enough, the police were right. His kidnappers, eventually caught, turned out to be Baader-Meinhof members. All Germans.

What is amazing is how a nation of honourable warriors were, in modern times, transformed into killers of women and children. Now they are the greatest pacifists in Europe, worse even than the Dutch and Danes. Winston Churchill was right when he said that the Germans are either at your throat or at your feet.

When, in October of 1940, Italy invaded Greece, Germany did not declare war on us. I remember the first victory against the Italians as if it were yesterday. The church bells began to ring, and continued to ring throughout. People poured out on to the streets hugging and kissing each other. My mother took my brother and myself out on to the verandah so we could witness the memorable spectacle. Both my father and uncle were at the front, and both had already been mentioned in dispatches. I remember my mother crying constantly, worried about her husband and brother, but I knew that she had nothing to worry about. A victory against great odds at Koritsa (Albania) does things to a four-year-old that defy description. When our army followed with another win against Mussolini at Tepeleni, I knew that Greece simply could never, ever, lose. All day long I would listen to the radio that extolled martial values and heroic deeds, and at night my mother would take us to the cinema to watch the newsreels. Courage on the battlefield became the *raison d'être*. It has stayed with me ever since, despite my battles having been fought mostly in seedy nightclubs.

After Mussolini's legions had been pushed back to the sea, Hitler came to his rescue. By April, the front had collapsed and our boys had been routed. The Germans, however, treated the army with enormous respect. As a symbolic gesture they allowed many officers to keep their swords, and the German high command praised the Greek soldier's tenacity and fighting spirit. The French had been beaten in six weeks, the Dutch in six days, but little Greece had fought both Italy and Germany and held out for six months. I remember a *Life* magazine headline that read, 'Greece, who taught the world how to live, is now teaching it how to die.' They were heady days for me, and I was as proud as a peacock.

Part of our house was requisitioned by the German officer corps and my father instructed us to have minimum contact with them. They were all extremely polite to us, of noble bearing and handsome to a man. They loved my brother and me because we spoke their language, and because all we asked them about was war and more war. Their favourite was my brother, however, who was ash blond, chubby and could sing 'Ach Du Lieber Augustine' in a high falsetto voice while accompanying himself on the piano.

Needless to say, my father exploited to the hilt his children's popularity with the occupiers. Once a week, my brother and I would deliver his underground resistance newspaper, *Greek Blood*, straight from the presses hidden inside his textile factory. My mother would have kittens every time it happened, but there was really no risk. The old man knew that no German would look inside the schoolbooks of two well-dressed lads who spoke German better than most Germans, especially when one of the two was a paradigm of Hitler's Aryan dream boy.

In 1942 my father received an order from Cairo to blow up the German headquarters, housed in the ESPO building in downtown Athens. Allied Intelligence had got word that the Germans had broken the resistance code, and hundreds of names were about to be circulated for arrest. The explosives expert that my father picked for the job was a young man named Perrikos. He succeeded brilliantly; the whole building was destroyed, along with its record. But in two days Perrikos was arrested by the Germans and tortured to death. He never revealed my father's name – who had already gone into hiding – nor did Perrikos give them the merest hint that the order had come from above. He went to his death claiming he had acted alone.

As to why he was caught in the first place, the horrible truth eventually leaked out. Perrikos had been betrayed by Communists inside the underground because of his political beliefs. He was pro-English, pro-King of Greece and pro-West. Communists in the resistance movement may have been anti-German, but they were just as eager to get rid of anyone who might give them trouble after the war, and Perrikos would have.

One night in the summer of 1965 I had just arrived at a chic Athenian nightclub only to discover that my usual table was occupied by a group of young unknowns. When I demanded that the *maître d'* remove the upstarts, one of the young men began to protest vehemently. In fact I heard him saying, 'Who does Theodoracopulos think he is?', at which point I asked him his name, since he already seemed to know mine. 'Perrikos' was the answer. He was the son of the man who had died so we could go on living.

Not very long after the incident I decided that my life as a whole and my attitude in particular left a lot to be desired. I like to think I've never pulled rank on anyone since but, in attempting to avoid it, I've often found myself attacking the rich and powerful in my various columns simply because they are rich and powerful. I was once labelled a 'terrorist among the rich'. If I am, the encounter with the son of Perrikos has had a lot to do with it.

· *21 December 1984* ·

This morning I have my first visit from my lawyer. It goes without saying that Sir David Napley, my solicitor, is far too grand to visit jailbirds and has sent a junior to represent him. I don't really mind, as I haven't much to say to Sir David, or to anyone else in the legal profession at the moment. The only thing that bothers me is that the junior has not brought any cigarettes with him, the only illegality the warders turn a blind eye to.

To me, the legal system in England seems almost as tangled a web as the class structure. Given the fact that people are forever suing me for the things I write, I guess I should consider myself irresponsible for not knowing the law inside out, but I figure the more one knows about the laws of libel the less one writes the truth. The perfect example is the fifteen-million-dollar libel suit brought against me by one Richard Golub, a New York lawyer who is married to the starlet Marisa Berenson. In a 1982 *Esquire* column, I had mentioned Golub as being brash, friendly at times beyond any previous justification and ready to spill his innermost thoughts about himself in order to sound hip. Back to reticence, was my message, and I only used Golub as an example because he had indeed once sat next to Alexandra and, without knowing her at all, told her things I would not tell a shrink.

I had nothing against Golub, except that he was an egregious social climber and somewhat of a bully. I made clear in my column that his 'spilling the beans' was a pose, and that so many New Yorkers – and Californians, for that matter – expose their inner thoughts as much as they do only because it's considered trendy. That is all.

Well, that was not all. Golub sued *Esquire* for fifteen big ones, and when the magazine defended the case rather than give him an apology, he decided to sue me, also. (As of this writing, January 1987, the case has been thrown out of two courts, yet I have been forbidden by my lawyers to mention his name while the case has been pending. Which means that an unscrupulous lawyer can sue non-stop, denying me the freedom of speech, costing me money to defend myself, while not wasting a penny on his part.) *Esquire* requires a writer to hand in his copy at least three months in advance, and the legal department goes through it with a fine comb. There is also a fact-checking department and one has to give names of people who witnessed the events one writes about. In the Golub case, the lawyers had cleared the copy without even having asked me any questions, something they do when there is any doubt on their part. Ditto on the fact-checking. I had all my witnesses ready and they all confirmed that Golub had indeed indulged in psychobabble. It made no difference, however. American society is a litigious one, and there is nothing more litigious than an American lawyer who has been exposed as a social climber and a bore.

Personally, I have never come close to suing anyone. I don't believe writers should sue, especially when they dish it out as much as I do. Nevertheless, I was amazed after Victor Kovner, the brilliant lawyer who represented *Esquire* and me against Golub, told me that even if the case took ten years to come to court and even if Golub had no case at all, which he didn't, I could not write anything about him until it was all over. I remember telling Victor that there must be a law that protects people from litigious lawyers, and Victor smiled and said that the Constitution and the Bill of Rights had thought of mostly everything but that.

In Golub's case, I would have written what I wrote even if I had known the laws inside out. As it turned out, I had not libelled him, therefore my instincts were correct. I told the truth and the truth turned out not to be libellous. In America, that is. Here in England, of course, the truth is not necessarily a defence. If the truth exposes someone to ridicule, it is considered a libel. Mind you, it is not as cut and dried as all that, but it is nevertheless much harder for a writer to write the truth over here than it is over there.

The same applies to court procedure. Judges run a very tight ship and lawyers at times give the impression they are more concerned with decorum than with getting their client's message across. Nothing is more frustrating than sitting in an English court of law, listening to a bewigged barrister drone on about how something one wrote has brought ridicule and shame upon his client, and how only a vast amount of money can restore his client's self-respect and peace of mind. And English judges can be merciless when the decorum of the court is breached. A writer friend of mine once yelled 'Hurray!' upon being judged not guilty by a jury, and the judge immediately sentenced him to one day in jail for contempt. My friend lost his temper, and recklessly said, 'Why don't you make it two, you bewigged buffoon?' to which the bewigged one answered by giving him thirty days in the pokey.

In Greece, court decorum is, as yet, an unheard-of phenomenon. Lawyers scream and interrupt, friends and relatives of litigants ditto, and the general court scene is one of chaos. A Greek judge once told me that emotional truth is more important than the facts, and that is the reason a carnival-like atmosphere prevails. By this I assume he meant that a judge can get to the real truth by examining people's emotions, but I don't buy that any more than I buy the Gestapo-like atmosphere in English courts.

Still, I am no stranger to Greek courts of law.

Alas, I know them only too well. In fact, it was in a Greek court that I first received a prison sentence, eighteen months for criminal libel.

It all came about when a small circulation English language daily, the *Athens News*, published the name and home address of Richard Welch, the American CIA station chief in Athens. There was a mighty anti-American spirit prevailing at the time – as there is to this day – and by his actions Yannis Horn, the editor and owner of the paper, virtually guaranteed that Welch's days were numbered.

Sure enough, he was murdered by unknown assassins soon after, a fact that led me to do some investigating of my own as to the reasons why Horn had published the unfortunate man's name and home address. What I got was not the 'smoking gun' kind of proof, but enough for me to write that Horn was under orders from foreign powers to expose Welch. I also discovered that Horn had been given the name of the KGB station chief in Athens, but had refused to publish it.

After my article appeared, Horn sued me for criminal libel. I, in turn, took my father's advice and engaged a high-powered and influential lawyer to defend me. What I didn't know at the time, however, was that my lawyer was up for a government post. Once the trial began, though, it became obvious that he was not about to go against the witnesses Horn had assembled, most of whom were people in the government. The kangaroo court lasted only one day and I got eighteen months in jail. I appealed and in due time the decision was not only reversed, but was declared null and void. Two years later, the *New York Times* Greek correspondent in Athens, Paul Anastasi, had a somewhat similar experience, and as of this writing his case is still pending. He, too, came to the conclusion that parts of the Greek press were being financed by foreign powers – namely the Soviet Union – and he, too, suffered from a kangaroo court's findings. Thank God the Appeals Court, however, still functions.

This afternoon I pay my first visit to the library. When I say 'library', I mean three cells whose connecting walls have been knocked down and approximately two thousand books placed inside. The preponderance of the reading material – detective stories and Westerns. The three cons who run the library are overtly homosexual, and all three are in for drugs. One of them, Jerry, seems to know who I am, and is extremely helpful while I look for books that people have not masturbated into. He tells me that most books are 'damaged' through masturbation, although there is nothing in their content to induce such reactions. 'I guess people in here just hate books,' is the way Jerry explains the phenomenon. My reaction is to say that it's better than burning them, but not by much. I take out a long, out-of-print book on the history of the world, and thank Jerry for the tips he gave me. Upon returning to my cell and being locked up, I am informed that tomorrow I'm being moved to C-wing, to a cell of my own as befits the orderly of the gym. I am beside myself with anticipation and happiness, as the Loon's night-time habits are becoming intolerable.

· *22 December 1984* ·

The only good thing about prison is the moving. Unlike the outside, here I am not burdened with material possessions; the physical act of moving is accomplished painlessly and immediately. This morning, after breakfast, I gather my two blankets, my two sheets, my one pillowcase, my extra pair of trousers, extra shirt, underwear and pair of socks, as well as my toothbrush, razor, soap, shaving cream, comb and tiny wooden mirror, and simply walk down my landing and up to landing 5, C-wing. Despite my pleas, I'm not allowed to take my plastic utensils or my potty. On account of some bureaucratic quirk prisoners are supposed to leave them behind, for the next inmate who will come in. I was just beginning to feel at home with them, but now I have to start getting used to the new ones all over again. If only they *were* new.

Although I am finally in a cell on my own, my joy is short-lived. The cell has dirty brown walls and the light is dim, making it hard to read. I begin to panic as I realize that, if I cannot read, the next three months will seem like three hundred. The worst part is the WC. There is only one toilet, one basin and one tap. There is no water pressure, making it almost impossible to wash the grease and grime off the utensils I've inherited. I do not have the courage even to look at the potty.

The screws, too, leave something to be desired. One of

them, Officer Williams, doesn't unlock me when the bell
rings for work as he notices that my cell is messy and my
bed undone. When I explain to him that I've just moved
in, he grunts and tells me that I won't be unlocked until
lunchtime. I try to explain further, but Williams, a big
brute of a man, slams the door shut and walks away. I sit
on the edge of the bed, feeling very sorry for myself, until
anger at the injustice of it sets in.

At moments like these, one feels that prison is a form of
retribution, and that no possible good can come from it.
I've only been inside for a week or so, and yet I feel that
I've got something in common with the rest of the inmates:
the criminal act I committed to get me in here and the
loathing of the structure of control that I have learned in
the slammer. Williams's attitude has suddenly made me
hate a system I've defended for so long. I try and imagine
what the others are going through. If they had jobs, they
will have lost them, if they had skills, they will be abandoned, if they had loved ones, they have the worry that
they will not be around when they are freed. If I am
worried about these things, I, doing a mere four months, I
hate to think what the other poor buggers must be suffering. If judges were to sentence people to the consequences
of a prison sentence there would be an international
outcry.

These thoughts remind me of what Ernest Van Den
Haag said to me before I came to Pentonville. Ernest is an
elderly gentleman, a professor of law and psychology at
Fordham University, and a writer of note. I first met
Ernest at a round-table discussion at the Lehrman In-
stitute, a group that meets regularly, chaired by Lewis
Lehrman, the tycoon who was the unsuccessful candidate
for governor of New York in 1982. Ernest knew all about
prison, having served two years – six months of which

were in solitary confinement – in one of Mussolini's jails for anti-fascist activities. The professor told me that the two years had gone by as if they were two weeks, probably because (as he put it) 'I felt very proud to be inside, like a hero, and the more they threw at me, the more heroic I felt.' He added that he was also young at the time, that youth can get used to anything.

I think of Ernest as I sit on the edge of the bed, because my anger has not only made the time go by quickly, but also stopped me feeling sorry for myself. Now I am only angry. I guess that's how dissidents can get through so many years of jail and torture without breaking. They are innocent to begin with, and, like saints who choose their martyrdom, feel only contempt for their keepers and no sorrow for themselves. Although it is hardly my case, it's still a lesson well learned this morning. When one is punished unjustly, the punishment is not really felt. Still, being spoiled, I am already longing for the safety of D-wing, the understanding of Mr Wrigley, the friendliness of Sid, even the company of Tony the Loon.

In the afternoon I go to the gym and tell Mr Leggett and Mr Heavy why I missed the morning session. They say nothing at all. Screws do not criticize other screws and never believe what cons tell them. On my way back, while the evening slop-out is taking place, an American with bushy hair and a heavy New York accent approaches me, shakes my hand and cheerfully welcomes me to the penthouse, as he calls it, because we are on the highest landing of C-wing. He's in for fraud, a fraud he claims he never committed, and he shows me a picture of his house and farm in Sussex. I believe him.

· *23 December 1984* ·

Christmas is two days away, and I would have liked to give a present to the three men who were kind to me while I was in D-wing – Mr Wrigley, Mr Holliday and Sid – but I have nothing. The deadening effects of materialism will not interfere in my relationship with those men. Which perhaps is a blessing in disguise. I think about this as I jump up and dress quickly, to avoid another confrontation with Williams. It is the first time since I was a very small child that people will have to take me at face value. I have nothing more in my pocket than the next guy, and it's a funny feeling. And not necessarily a bad one.

Yesterday went slowly and today is just as bad. The single cell provides certain comforts of privacy, yet it makes the time drag ever so slowly. With a stranger, one lies awake, aware of every noise, every move, hoping that one's vigilance will pay dividends. Fear and anxiety are antidotes to boredom. But God, how slowly time passes once the door is banged shut and one is alone. The period from five in the evening until sleep comes, sometime around midnight, is the worst. Today I begin to walk diagonally across the 7′ by 13′ cell, day-dreaming and longing to exhaust myself, but to no avail. After freedom, sleep is the most cherished commodity in prison.

In the past, whenever I was stuck for time and under a deadline, I remember hankering for the uninterrupted solitude of a prison cell. Now that I have all the time in the world, I cannot get myself even to read. That we are allowed neither pen nor paper makes it easier to fool oneself and pretend that, if they were available, one would do nothing but worship the muse all day. And night.

This morning I give all my tobacco to the landing-cleaner of C-5, in return for a small bar of soap and some paper hankies, which he promises to provide after dinner. But when I look into his cell his things are gone and I realize that I've been had. On his last day, he lied in order to get my smokes, knowing that he had seven hours to go and I have seventy days. I make it a point never to trust anyone again. He seemed like a decent chap, even going to the trouble to ask me what soap I liked.

I chat with Harry, who occupies the cell next to mine. He is small, bald and has a gentle manner. He tells me he's thirty-eight, but he looks at least fifty. Harry has been inside for at least ten years and has been brought to Pentonville to finish his last twelve months. He's in for armed robbery, but claims he was only the lookout. He shows me a picture of his wife and children. She divorced him two years after he went in, and he hasn't seen the kids in over six years. I notice his cell is very neat, like his speech and manner. I feel extremely sorry for him, and wonder what will happen to him once he gets out. He gives me the impression of being homosexual, but perhaps it's because he is so gentle. I ask him if he's had bad times inside, and he smiles ruefully and says that everyone has bad times in prison.

The Christmas carols I hear over my tiny transistor make me gloomier than usual. Memories of happy times come once again flooding in, and I am sad, despairing. The

weather helps, however. There is no snow to remind me of
Gstaad and happier Christmases past. There's only rain
and more rain, and greyness.

· *24 December 1984* ·

The prison is emptying out as screws are leaving for home, and being filled to the brim with dossers and winos. Mostly elderly, they have nowhere to live and are generally so run-down that hospitals won't even take them in. For Christmas, these unfortunate souls throw a rock against a large department-store window or assault a policeman in order to get themselves arrested, thus ensuring three square meals a day during the hols. Everyone in prison lives in fear of having a dosser put in with them, and no one more than me as I have a single cell. The reason they're as feared as they are is obvious. They smell to high heaven, and although one's sense of smell is deadened after a couple of days living with the urine, the dossers have been known to make even old-timers throw up in disgust. Harry tells me that two years ago he had one die on him, and as he had just been locked up for the night he had to wait almost twelve hours before he was unlocked and the body taken out.

That is all I need for Christmas, I tell myself, and then discover that landing 4 of C-wing has broken pipes, so our solitary toilet will have to accommodate an extra seventy-five men this morning.

After breakfast I'm told to report to the canteen to collect my week's wages. The canteen, like the library, is nothing more than two connecting cells with the middle wall missing. I have earned the princely sum of two pounds. The screw who doles out the money tells me that mine is the highest salary in the whole nick, a fact I find extremely ironic as I have never in my life been able to out-earn anyone, least of all two thousand crooks.

This small earning capacity has not endeared me to my fellow Greeks. I remember once, as a journalist, meeting a Greek politician and hearing him remark to one of his flunkeys that his friend John Theodoracopulos also had a son named Taki. When I told him the son and I were one and the same, he refused to believe it. He didn't, I later found out, because he simply could not imagine that the son of a shipowner and industrialist would be a lowly journalist. In fact, variations of this incident have taken place time and time again, since the majority of my countrymen look upon tycoons like, say, Aristotle Onassis, with the kind of reverence the Austrians reserve for such non-earners as Wolfgang Amadeus Mozart. The terrible thing is that even younger and younger generations of Greeks have not managed to break the mould. To be rich is considered not only to be more intelligent, but also worthy of more respect.

And to be, of course, above the law.

Here is a small example. In 1965, I was driving to La Bonne Auberge, a fancy restaurant in Antibes, with Alexander Onassis and another friend of his. Alexander, then about twenty years old, was driving like a maniac, four-wheel drifting the car around every corner and doing ninety miles an hour along the narrow Corniche that takes one to Antibes from Monte Carlo.

I was leery, but not about to ask a young man to slow down. I am Greek, and, among us, that would mean losing face. Just before Antibes he sideswiped a car and we had to pull over. The driver of the car we had hit was an older man, obviously shaken, with a Russian accent. He was almost apologetic, as if it were his fault. Alexander instantly smelled blood and began giving him a bad time. 'What's your name, buddy?' was the nicest thing he said to him.

'Serge Lifar,' came the answer.

When I realized who the man was I tried to interfere. I told Onassis that Lifar was a great artist, a ballet legend, obviously poor, and even reminded him that the whole thing was his, Alexander's, fault. Unfortunately, Lifar had neither a driver's licence nor any insurance. Onassis promptly decided to sue him and took down his name and particulars. Lifar almost got down on his knees, but Alexander knew he was on to a winner and refused.

Well, in the end, Onassis did not get his way. He tried to sue, but I testified in favour of Lifar and Alexander's case was dismissed. He never forgave me. Three years later he died in a tragic air crash. And today I speak ill of a young man long dead only because, during the argument with Lifar, I realized it wasn't Alexander's fault. He had no more idea what a moral education is than I have knowledge of Hebrew. No one had ever taught him anything to do with ethical values, generosity of spirit, even basic good manners. Both his father and mother spent their days in pursuit of money, power and pleasure, and never took time off to see the children learn anything except how fast cars and motor boats work.

Had Alexander and Christina gone to strict English boarding-schools, perhaps they would have turned out differently, but I doubt it. The Greeks have a terrible habit of bootlicking upwards, while pushing people around whom they consider their inferiors. This bullying trait derives from having been under the Ottoman Empire's yoke for almost four hundred years. From 1453 to 1827, to be precise. When Greece joined the European Community, back in 1981 I believe, I gave a small dinner and announced to my guests that we were, from that moment on, Europeans. Which meant we would no longer say 'I'm flying to Europe,' when travelling to Italy, play with worry beads, fear the state, evade taxes, resent authority, trust only our immediate family members, choose our children's husbands and wives or beat our women.

But four hundred years of occupation make habits hard to break. The modern Greek state has not helped matters. Retroactive laws are as common as scandals in Washington, thus making the Greek businessman insecure and mistrustful of the government. And there is also, of course, the historical background which sees the Greek with a deeply ingrained distrust of authority. Civil disobedience, considered right and good for four centuries, suddenly became a crime. Few Greeks understood this, back in 1827. More do at present, but the democratic and liberal ideas of the West are not yet part of Greek life. To the victor belong the spoils, and the victor for the Greek is the rich man.

The gym is closed, making time drag even more than usual. I do my knee-bends, push-ups and stretching exercises, but do not dare to lie on the floor and do stomach-crunches. The previous occupant has left tell-tale signs of excreta on the floor, dried out, like giant worm-casts. And the smell is everywhere of urine. This is the problem of inheriting a single cell. My next-door neighbour warned me that, during their last week inside, single-cell inmates don't ever bother to slop out at night, leaving as messy a cell as possible. This is not because they mistakenly believe that the screws will have to clean it up before the next prisoner occupies it. In fact, they know damn well that the next poor bastard will have to do it, but they delight in it anyway. One would think that the inmate going out would do anything to try and make the one coming in comfortable. But that is not the way life goes inside.

Yet, ironically, most sociologists believe that we imprison people in order to rehabilitate them. From my limited experience until now, prisoners instead get hardened while doing time, growing increasingly more convinced that they are unfortunate victims of their environment and that the system is stacked against them.

Which, I'm sure, is often true, but not at all as the two Rastafarians who chat me up in the gym every day claim it is. Both in for armed robbery and drug smuggling, they still seriously claim that they *had* to smuggle, in order to fight Mrs Thatcher's anti-black government. When I scoffed and reminded them that the majority of black Englishmen do not indulge in crime, they told me that I spoke like a white man who knows and understands nothing about blacks. *All* the blacks, they assured me, with the exception of a few 'collaborators' were ready to steal and kill to achieve a just society.

Shades of Eldridge Cleaver's bullshit of the sixties.

One or two hours go by while I grunt and groan through about three hundred push-ups and about the same number of knee-bends. I try to do about forty at a time, taking a short break in between. It may sound like a lot, but when one has nothing to do, three hundred push-ups are for the lazy.

I remember having read somewhere that a black prisoner doing life in a Trenton, New Jersey, jail had managed to get up to *ten thousand* a day, but I don't see how he could keep count. In karate class we try to do one thousand kicks once per week, but we only manage it because each man counts up to one hundred.

*

My first experience with lots of push-ups started with karate. Our Japanese instructor, Mr Okano, would walk into the dojo, bow to Sensei Funakoshi's picture (Mr Funakoshi is the father of modern-day karate) and then start counting, '*Ichi, ni, san, shi, go, roku, hichi, hachi, ku, ju,* etc.' all the way up to one hundred. While we did our push-ups, Mr Okano would walk around the class, carrying a large wooden Samurai sword. Whenever he saw someone dodging, he would whack him rather hard with it. The best way to avoid getting whacked was to do them, and the second best was to have one's arms trembling while keeping the body half-way between the floor and the uppermost position. I used that trick for a long time, until I realized that doing the true push-ups was easier. I once told Mr Okano that I had been cheating at the start, and he remembered it. He knew it was harder, so he let me cheat.

This was the year I took up the martial arts, 1964. I had seen an exhibition by Japanese instructors and became an instant believer. I ran and signed up in a dojo located on 56th Street and Lexington Avenue, on New York's upper East side. Karate was originally an empty-handed art of self-defence in which arms and legs were systematically trained to be used as weapons. The essence of the art was *kime*, or the focus of strength. A sudden explosion of technique coupled with power-producing speed.

The first purpose of the art was the nurturing of a sublime spirit, the spirit of humility through strength. But with the passing of the Samurai, or Bushido, philosophy and the coming of materialism, karate changed. The Americans were the first to spoil it by insisting on competition within certain rules, thus changing karate from a martial art into a sport. By 1964, then, karate had become the favourite sport of ethnic minorities in America, some of whom understood as much about humility and respect as Khomeini about compassion.

Mr Okano, my first teacher, was a traditionalist. He taught in the classical Japanese manner, which freely translated means teaching in a cruel way, but with a soft heart. I've had three karate *senseis* (teachers) in the twenty years I've been practising, and all three are like fathers to me, only more so. During my first months under Mr Okano, I noticed that the class kept getting smaller and smaller. Sometimes only I would show up. Finally the owner, a fat man who could have used some of the sit-ups we were doing non-stop, called Mr Okano into his office and told him the training was too tough for American students, and that he should let up. Apparently Mr Okano said, 'Ah, velly, velly good, weak students no good.' He continued to teach his way and was fired. The owner didn't care about turning the mostly black and Hispanic students into Samurais, he only wanted their weekly welfare cheque, with which most of them paid for their lessons. So I followed Mr Okano to the Land of the Rising Sun.

On the next to last day, a friend of mine from Greece dropped in to see what this karate I kept raving about actually was. He came in with a good-looking Spanish gentleman who is at present the King of Spain. He politely asked if he could join the class. I knew Juan Carlos from Monte Carlo and the tennis circuit, and was surprised to see him in a dojo atmosphere. Prince Juan Carlos had been issued a brown belt by an instructor in Spain, in the same spirit, I presume, that royalty is issued, awarded rather, medals for bravery. The mistake was that no one bothered to tell me different. I was only a white belt and eager to prove myself.

At the end of each class, Mr Okano would make us all stand against the wall; then he would point at two students, and they would fight. Needless to say, the Prince and I got the nod. Now I respect royalty and all that (well, not really, in fact not at all), but on this occasion I closed my eyes, screamed as hard as I could and charged. Poor Juan Carlos, he never really had a chance. Now, of course, he is the King of Spain, as romantic a title as one could wish for. And he's done a hell of a job. In fact, if it weren't for him, Spain would not be enjoying a democracy today.

His wife, Queen Sophia, is the sister of the ex-King of Greece, Constantine II. The Greek royal family and I have had our ups and downs, mostly downs, as I have never managed to learn the time-honoured custom of bowing and scraping to someone because of an accident of birth.

The last time time I saw her, in the summer of 1975, I was seated next to her during a grand lunch on board Stavros Niarchos's yacht, the *Atlantis*, off Majorca, where Juan Carlos has a summer place. The Greek Colonels, who had usurped power eight years earlier, were being tried, after having given up power voluntarily. Naturally the conversation concerned the result of the trial, and at one point Sophia turned to me and asked me my opinion. I said that I felt sorry that three patriotic officers, however crude and inefficient, had been condemned to death.

Perhaps it was an insensitive remark in view of the fact that her brother had lost his throne due to his opposition to their coup, but I truly felt for them. Greece has a tradition of attracting only poor and uneducated boys to the war college. There are no patrician soldiers in the birthplace of democracy, and the best and the brightest either go into the private sector or leave the country as early as possible. What the state does, then, is to recruit young, mostly uneducated farm boys from the poorest areas of an already poor land. Once recruited, they are indoctrinated for five years and then sent out to fight.

The Colonels whose power ended in 1974, had been recruited just after the Second World War. Their god was anti-Communism, and nothing else. Greece was in the middle of a civil war against Soviet-backed guerrillas. It does not take a genius to realize why the Colonels were what they were. Some of them had families butchered by the Reds, and their fear of Communism had increased their myopia when they grabbed power. There was no danger at the time, as we now realize, but every politician of the right, including the Palace, had been warning us to the contrary.

So the Colonels made a mess of it, but they had meant well and were honest. And inadvertently, after their fall, they managed to ensure that democracy was not taken for granted by the politicians.

Greece has had selective democracy at best since it became a free country in 1827. The state owns all public utilities, radio-telecommunications, television, airlines and all heavy industry. Businessmen traditionally have been shielded by government protection from competition, and have, in turn, helped politicians get rich. Although the press is supposedly free, it is nevertheless controlled through the government's monopoly on newsprint, by advertising decisions of government-dominated enterprises and by the issuing of licences for future projects.

The Greek royal family was instrumental in defeating the Communists after the Second World War. They rallied the pro-Western side and gave badly needed moral support to the army. While the civil war dragged on until 1951, the King ruled instead of reigned. That was normal. Unfortunately, though, this became a habit. And the politicians helped. Every ambitious pol made sure the King liked him, because a nod from the monarch meant automatic promotion. Constantine Karamanlis, the longest-serving prime minister in Greek history, leap-frogged everyone by being hand-picked by King Paul, the present King's father. But Karamanlis bit the hand that fed him. In fact, he bit it off.

I had grown up in this atmosphere of Versailles-like obedience to the crown, and I didn't like it one bit. So, when Sophia asked me what I felt about the Colonels, I told her the truth. There was a hush as jet-setters strained to hear more. She asked me to repeat myself, as if she hadn't heard correctly, and I did. She then called me a pest and turned her back to me.

Our host, Stavros Niarchos, was not only the richest Greek shipowner, he was also the deafest. That day his deafness came in handy. He pretended to have heard nothing. But Sophia insisted. 'I dare you to say this to my brother,' she went on.

'I will, if His Majesty asks me,' was all I said. Everyone, however, considered my answer *lèse-majesté*. I could feel the rest of the jet-setters distancing themselves from me. Her brother, to his credit, came up to me after lunch and told me that I had the right to my opinion. He also said it to Sophia. My only thought was, what a pity it took his losing the throne to learn a rather simple fact of life. If he had known that before, Greece would be a hell of a lot better off now.

· *25 December 1984* ·

Breakfast today is a feast. Tea with toast, plus cornflakes and one egg. Later, after slop-out, we all receive our presents from the governor of the jail: one packet of butter, a bag of sugar and a cake. The governor also sends us his best wishes for Christmas, but does not add his best wishes for a prosperous New Year for us all.

We are allowed to loiter around the landing for about fifteen minutes; since it's raining, there is no exercise period in the yard. I go over and visit George, the American who lives just across from me and who is fighting extradition to the States for alleged fraud, the same offence that has landed him in Pentonville. I give him my butter and sugar in return for some magazines. George is a nice enough fellow, but strange. 'I know Oleg Cassini,' is the first thing he tells me on this holiest of days. George thinks that armed robbers get the most respect in jail, which makes my crime – as well as his – akin to being a male nurse in General George Patton's army. (Which, incidentally, was Andreas Papandreou's job during the Second World War. In Florida, of all places, where he had gone to evade the draft back in the old country.)

The old country seems to be constantly on my mind since I became Her Majesty's guest. Like the very old, I can remember every detail of long ago, but not of the recent past. Today I rack my brain trying to recall a worse Christmas, but to no avail. The closest is the Christmas of 1944, when the Communist guerrillas decided to take over by force of arms. They managed to overrun most of Athens, butchering the unarmed populace in the process, but, typically, they failed to take Kolonaki, the ritziest part of town. Our house was very near the British embassy, and the Greek police and the few British Red Berets defended it to the last.

My father, ever the opportunist, had acquired an armoured personnel carrier from an Italian officer in exchange for a suit of clothes one year earlier. That was when Italy had surrendered, and the furious Germans were rounding up the occupying Italian officers and sometimes shooting them on sight. Daddy hid the APC in one of his idle factories; when the Reds made their move, he crossed the battle lines and parked it in front of our house.

When the shooting started, my brother and I were on the ground floor having a piano lesson. The lady teaching us insisted that Christmas was the perfect day for lessons, as our heads would not be cluttered with school matters. But when she heard the first shot, she threw herself underneath the piano and remained there for the duration. My brother Harry and I burst out laughing. Having endured four years of constant bombing by the Allies, the noise of machine-gun fire hardly registered. But a fat lady cowering underneath a grand piano was an incredibly funny sight. We were still laughing when a young British soldier came flying through a window, mortally wounded as it turned out, having been hit by sniper fire. He wore a red beret and was very blond. Our mother covered our eyes so we would not see a young man die.

Often people accuse me of being too right-wing, but I am nothing of the kind. What I *am* is passionately anti-

Communist, as well as deeply suspicious of liberals who believe one can deal with 'Commies'. The Greek Communist Party has not changed since 1944. The paroxysms of rage induced in them by Nicholas Gage's book *Eleni* – a compelling account of the tragic persecution, torture and execution of his mother by the Communists – is proof that the Greek Reds are not only unwilling to admit past crimes, but only too eager to besmirch the memory of the thousands they murdered by calling them Fascists. (There was no CIA at the time, otherwise they'd all be accused of being agents of Uncle Sam.)

Whenever political discussions come up, I cannot help but think of my father's factory workers who were murdered for committing the ultimate crime: working for a capitalist. The irony is that very few rich died during the civil war. We knew enough about Uncle Joe Stalin's followers to have prepared ourselves. So it was the priests, teachers and poor farmers who suffered the most. And, of course, those who remained loyal to their employees, like my old man.

The ghastliest of all, however, was that poor 'Tommy' paratrooper – to have survived action against the Germans, only to die in a rich man's drawing room from an 'Allied' bullet in the back.

Mr Leggett and Mr Heavy bring me three mince pies and a bottle of lime, which I devour almost immediately. They also bring me a Christmas card and a forbidden pack of ciggies. After a dinner of turkey and more goodies, the Salvation Army singers are heard carolling away. But they are soon drowned out by inmates yelling 'Fuck off' in unison. Poor Salvation Army volunteers. They leave their houses to bring some cheer to criminals and perverts, and they get told to fuck off. I feel for them, but I also understand why everyone is outraged. We all want the day to be over, and we don't want to think about it while waiting for it to pass. And it's the longest one yet. I imagine my children and Alexandra asleep in America, or opening presents, and get more depressed.

· *26 December 1984* ·

Suddenly, after breakfast, a screw I've never seen before comes into my cell and tells me I've got two minutes to pack my belongings. 'You're moving,' he barks. I try to tell him that there must be some mistake, but he smirks and gives me the choice of moving quietly or going to the punishment cells. My mind races. Am I being let out? Or is it that prick Williams giving me a rough time? Or am I being transferred to an open prison, a 'country-club' jail?

I gather all my meagre belongings, plus my two sheets, one pillowcase, two blankets, my books and clothes. I try to take my utensils with me and, most loved object of all, my potty, but the screw, who is watching me like a hawk, orders me to leave those behind. He marches me out, down the landing and one stairway and on to D-wing again, but not to my old landing, but D-4, cell 30. Which means I'm now on landing number 4, and in cell number 30.

To my utter horror, the cell is in a state of such filth that even the screw seems embarrassed. The two beds are both covered with excrement, the walls with dirty graffiti, and the potties which have been thrown aside are still full of human excrement. The smell of urine is all at once unbearable, so I turn and plead that the screw allows me to see a superior officer. He says nothing in response and just walks out, slamming the door shut behind him. I rack my brain as to why this is happening to me, and finally conclude that it's because I was rude to Williams. But perhaps I am just becoming paranoid and it's nothing to do with him. And here I thought I was being sent to an open prison.

I spend the rest of the morning standing up against the door, too disgusted by the squalor to touch or go near anything. The only move I make is towards the window. I pry it open and after a while the smell seems to be going away. I decide to wait until they unlock me for lunch, and then make a dash for Mr Wrigley's office. If he's not there and I'm ordered back to the cell, I will refuse and go to the punishment block. My only fear is that the block might be in the same state as D-4, cell 30, but I doubt it. Nothing could be worse than this.

A prison is supposed to be like a huge factory. Its purpose is to produce respectable citizens from the raw material of convicted offenders. But it differs from even the most incompetent factory in its failure to turn out a standard law-abiding, considerate, child-rearing, job-holding model. How can anyone in his right mind believe that the animals who have left the cell I'm now supposed to live in can possibly become useful citizens, mortgage-payers, fathers, even warders? They will be back here soon, and for once I hope to God I can repay the favour.

Eventually I'm unlocked and head straight for Mr Wrigley's office. It's shut. I go to Mr Holliday and tell him of my predicament. I've got tears in my eyes. He sympathizes with me, and tells me to skip dinner and get a mop and go to work. The Augean stables come to mind, but I ain't no Hercules. Eventually, however, I manage to achieve some kind of order. I spend the rest of the day scrubbing, and even manage to get a pair of rubber gloves from a kind kitchen inmate to help me clean out the potty. I toss and turn all night, wondering what's in store for me, and why things have come to this.

· *27 December 1984* ·

Still no word from the powers that be as to why I've been moved. Every time I hear keys jangling, my heart leaps. I am expecting a cellmate any minute and, judging by the cell I've been assigned to, my next roomie is bound to be a dosser, I'm afraid. There is only one thing left to do. Escape.

I am not seriously contemplating escaping, but thinking about it gives one hope. The only way out of this place is to hide underneath the van that takes prisoners on remand to the courts each day. Apparently, the search is random, and, if one is lucky, one may just make it. Still, the last con to escape from Pentonville managed it during the bombing of the Second World War. The walls are too thick to dig through, and ever since Her Majesty began serving us with plastic utensils even those efforts are futile.

There is no gym today, and no workshops, so I spend the morning cleaning up as best I can. Good old Sid comes to the rescue yet again. He brings me a brand-new potty, lots of detergent and a new mop. I have to return the latter – it's considered a weapon by the authorities – but I put it to good use for more than an hour. I have been given a form letter for the governor and spend some time explaining to him that, despite having been a model prisoner until now, I have been assigned to live in a lavatory, and a dirty lavatory at that.

Strange as it seems, the moment I hand in the letter and look around my cell, the place starts to grow on me. It is amazing what six hours of scrubbing will do to the filthiest of places. Even more amazing is how quickly one gets acclimatized to one's surroundings, once inside.

In jail you learn to separate your few possessions in case of robbery. I hide one pack of cigarettes inside my extra shirt, the other behind my books. My soap is ingeniously hidden in my pocket, which, needless to say, has no money in it. I find it funny to have soap instead of money in my pockets, just as I find it funny that the manual work I did cleaning up my cell has exhausted me and put me to sleep faster than any exercise session – far more gruelling – has up to now. I guess there is something to be said about an honest day's work, after all.

· *28 December 1984* ·

I find it hard to believe, but things get worse as soon as I wake up. An officer comes into my cell and informs me that I am no longer the gym orderly. I have been assigned to workshop number 3, which means I shall be sewing buttons for army uniforms. I have also taken a pay-cut to one pound per week. The reason for this is that the Home Office has instructed the prison authorities that I am a security risk, and likely to try to escape. It is as if my day-dreaming of yesterday has been monitored by Big Brother over at Westminster.

After breakfast, I go down to the bowels of the prison and begin doing what the majority of people the world over do for the greater part of their lives. The workshop is a long, rectangular room with grey walls, bright, overhead neon lights and sewing-machines screwed into wooden benches. About one hundred inmates are assigned to this particular shop.

A supervisor shows me how to work the machine, hands me some jackets and tells me the quota I need to hand in during the three-hour morning session. After a couple of hours I am hopelessly behind it, but so are the three cons working alongside me on the same bench. I guess this is why capitalism works and socialism does not. Although falling behind will cost me privileges and a further pay-cut, the lack of incentive makes it difficult to concentrate.

At best, the work is shoddy, as I have nothing to gain if I work harder than the next guy. So I day-dream away, trying to figure out who has it in for me at the Home Office, and cursing the day I took my first snort of cocaine.

Warren is a large black man who is doing two years for fraud. He was a rock promoter who collected money for a concert and then absconded with the loot. Warren tells me that the thing he misses most is women, and when I ask him how many women he misses, he answers that he lives with three, but is actually servicing about seven, or rather *was*. Warren is convinced that after his women experience his lovemaking they are incapable of ever going with another man; thus, by keeping him in jail, the state is punishing seven innocent ladies. He plans to use this theory for his appeal, which must be a first.

Warren also believes that by making us sew army jackets, the state is using forced labour *à la* Hitler, and that these very jackets will one day help the English imperialists to suppress his people back in Jamaica. Despite his bullshit, I like Warren a lot. All his teeth are gold, and what's more the Queen herself has paid for them. Apparently, every guest of Her Majesty has the right to have new teeth put in, and the smart ones demand gold teeth, which they sell as soon as they get out. Not a bad scam, when you think of it.

When the bell rings, we are searched, marched back to the cells and given a random check before dinner. It has been a very long morning. I look back at the halcyon days when I was the gym orderly, and almost want to weep.

· *29 December 1984* ·

During slop-out this morning, I hear from Warren that a man has hanged himself in his cell. I get this confirmed later by Frank Heavy, who has come in to see me and tell me he's sorry I no longer work in the gym.

Later Warren tells me that the screws have been known to leak false information to inmates they dislike, such as the death of loved ones, or impending divorce, and prisoners have been known to hang themselves as a result. I guess if I were doing years and heard that something had happened to my kids, the resulting depression would be enough to have me contemplating suicide, but I doubt it. I hope I never find out.

Warren works very slowly, almost as slowly as I do, and keeps a non-stop chatter going. Talking is illegal, but he manages it without getting caught. Lots of cons know how to do it, but it's hard to understand how. Women apart, Warren's favourite subject is drugs. Cocaine, to be exact. Warren thinks it's the best thing this side of heaven, and insists I'm a fool not to miss it. His women bring him a stash every visit. He sells some and smokes the rest. It has more effect that way, he tells me, but when I ask him how he keeps all the paraphernalia that goes along with smoking coke, he gets suspicious and changes the subject.

The afternoon session is shorter than the morning's, but somehow it seems longer. Time drags as never before. I think of the millions of women who have to do this type of work in order to live, and for the first time I understand the inhumanity of the Industrial Revolution. I'd prefer to be in a chain gang digging ditches any day of the year. Warren agrees.

The closest I have ever been to a factory assembly line was back in 1959, in the Sudan. My father had read in a newspaper that the Sudan imported cloth despite being one of the world's greatest cotton producers, coals to Newcastle in other words, so off he went to Khartoum, and in no time at all he built a thirty-million-dollar air-conditioned textile mill, the largest in the Middle East, with 3000 looms, 55,000 spindles and 5000 workers. It was called Sudan-American Textile Industry, as Washington had loaned him ten million big ones.

Work began in 1957 and was completed two years later. Just as the factory began operations I got myself in a spot of financial bother in New York. I had a girlfriend then named Linda Christian, the ex-wife of Tyrone Power and one of the great beauties of her time. Linda, besides being a beauty, had other attributes, too. Like being one of the greatest spenders of all time. When I could no longer keep up with the bills, I had the brilliant idea of taking all the family silver and selling it to a silversmith. I did this while my parents were in Greece. Upon their return I owned up just as they were about to call the fuzz, but told them I had lost the money gambling. That was even stupider than selling the stuff, because my father's younger brother had committed suicide when, at a very young age, he had lost at cards in his club and could not pay within twenty-four hours, as was then customary. I did not know this when I made up the gambling story and could not get my old man to believe me when I finally told the truth.

After my crime, Sudan was the perfect place for me and I was duly dispatched there by a furious old man who warned me I had to stay there for two years, non-stop. My mother as usual tried to help me, but the old boy was adamant. He even rang President Abboud and asked him to make sure I did not leave the country until he, my father, said I could.

Once there, however, things turned out to be not at all bad. Khartoum was not as cosmopolitan as Cairo, but it had a charm and a quality of life to be found nowhere else in that part of the world. In fact, it was Durrell country. I was given a large house on the Nile, complete with swimming pool and tennis court, a driver and a car and an unlimited allowance in Sudanese piastres. The European community welcomed me with open arms, and I began the pursuit of the good life almost immediately.

My circle of friends, too, was straight out of Durrell. There was Grace Contomichalos, a Levantine beauty married to a rich Greek cotton merchant, who was Justine personified. Bill Wild, a Yul Brynner lookalike, was the CIA station chief in Khartoum and, like the rest of us, in love with Grace. Baron Gottfried von Cramm, the ex-husband of Barbara Hutton, and one of the greatest tennis players of all time, was my tennis partner, and an assortment of young English and French civil servants made up our group. I spent the mornings playing tennis at the Omdurman tennis club, my afternoons swimming at various pools and the nights at the Gordon club, an open-air nightclub frequented by Europeans. Every weekend I flew to Cairo for more sophisticated fun, and was back in Khartoum by Monday morning.

But it all came to a sudden end when my father arrived unannounced and saw for himself what I was up to. I was immediately exiled from my exile and sent to Greece, where he swore I would get on one of his ships for the next decade. I managed to avoid that fate by stopping over in Switzerland and breaking my leg in thirteen places while racing a friend on a bet. The old man took pity on me, and I never came close to working again. The Sudan factory was nationalized by the government that followed that of President Abboud, and I still remember my father telling me the writing was on the wall when a Sudanese politician had poor von Cramm thrown out of the country because Gottfried had complained about the lack of modern plumbing in Khartoum. I have never returned to the Sudan, but looking back at the six months I spent there, it seems to be as happy a period as my days in the gym. As the philosopher said, it's all relative.

· *30 December 1984* ·

As Sydney Smith so wisely put it, toleration never had a present tense. I think of Sydney as I pace up and down the cell waiting to be released for slop-out. Today there is no work, which should make one feel glad, but strangely it doesn't. I hope to hear from the governor why I've been deemed a security risk, but I am not exactly holding my breath. The bureaucracy of a prison is as bad as that of Washington, and I have no illusions about my case being heard.

It burns me up thinking about it, however. It does not make sense for the Home Office to think I would try and escape. In fact, it's ludicrous. I'm doing four months, not four years, and had permission to leave the country while awaiting sentencing, yet showed up in court of my own free will. So why would I think of escaping now?

My cell is very draughty, and I think I'm starting a cold. All I need now is to feel sick, just so I can finish up the year in the manner I've lately become accustomed to.

· *31 December 1984* ·

The last day of a disastrous year.

It dawns in typical fashion, as if the gods are trying to tell me something I already know. Grey, gloomy, wet, depressing. After three weeks of trying, I am the first to reach the loo and slop out this morning. It is a good omen, I am told. I'm not so sure, however, because just as I am in the process of slopping out, a rat jumps out from the waste-bin and disappears among the rushing inmates.

After breakfast I go to see Mr Wrigley – who by now thinks I'm a con man because of the Home Office instructions – and ask permission to go to landing number 1 and say goodbye to Sid. The old boy is getting out today, although, as Mr Wrigley tells me, he should be back in a month or two, since poor Sid has no other family than people like us. 'Send the Rolls for me and we'll have lunch at the Ritz,' is what he has to say in bidding me goodbye, and I feel as if I'm losing my closest friend. Which I am.

Later on, two Rastafarians get into a fight with a couple of Irish boys in the workshop. The Rastas are thin and tall, the Irish short and muscular, and the fight is no contest. Prison rules state that no guard should try and break up a fight unless there is a 2:1 ratio of screws to inmates. While the alarm bells ring and the supervisor locks himself inside his cage, I watch the two Irish lads push the black guys around pretty badly, kick them once they're down and about to inflict real damage, when every black in the workshop comes to the Rastas' aid. They are lynching the Irishmen, and all we do is sit and watch. When, panting and sweating, the guards arrive, they break it up, but one Irishman has his eyeball hanging from a thread. It's hideous to see, and grotesque to have taken no part in separating them, but such are the lessons one learns in prison. Don't get involved unless your property is threatened. Or your life. It is exactly the opposite of the Christian ethic, but it's the golden rule while inside.

I don't know why the fight started or who started it, but I did see Black Solidarity at work. Warren tells me he was trying to break it up, but he forgets that I do have almost perfect vision and saw him put the boot in, as they say. Literally. Tempers are frayed today, as always during special days.

An older Pakistani man who works two benches down tells me a funny story during a cigarette break in the bathroom. A professional pickpocket, he was working the Regent Palace Hotel in Piccadilly when he picked up a briefcase from a man paying his bill and disappeared with it into Hyde Park. Once in the park he opened it up and found a bomb ticking away. He raced away and was almost immediately tackled by Special Branch detectives who had been following him ever since he picked it up. They thought it was a transfer between conspirators. He had spent three months sticking to his story, and then another six waiting for trial. He then got two years. If his story is true, he's the unluckiest pickpocket in London.

The supervisor is once again complaining about my lack of output, and I tell him that I have no experience with machines. 'You're the worst I've ever seen,' he tells me, and I can't help asking him if Oscar Wilde (who spent two nights in Pentonville) was any better. 'If you think I keep records of who comes in here, you're mistaken,' he answers.

And so the last day of the year nears its end in a workshop, sewing buttons for army jackets, talking to a man who's never heard of Oscar Wilde.

After the 4.30 p.m. tea, which is what dinner is euphemistically called in Pentonville, the countdown begins. As the hour before midnight approaches, the noise level becomes intolerable. Unlike Christmas Eve, which everyone tried to ignore, New Year's Eve is an opportunity for every con to scream his lungs out. Most of the yelling is racially motivated, and extremely lewd. But at least it keeps me from thinking about past eves. One thing does cross my mind, however, and makes me smile to myself. Tomorrow will be the first time in exactly twenty-eight years that I shall wake up on New Year's Day without a terrible hangover.

· *1 January 1985* ·

This morning, for the first time, I feel the worst is over. From now on it is only a matter of time and patience. There are certain psychological barriers while one is 'doing bird', as they say in prison, the obvious ones being birthdays of loved ones, holidays and so on. For me, the next big one is getting to the half-way point. After that, they tell me, it's all downhill. At the moment, I feel I'm starting on the second lap of the four-lap mile.

While I wait to be unlocked, it occurs to me that this is not the first New Year's Day I've spent in the clink. Back in 1954, during the Christmas holidays, my father had taken me along with him to Palm Beach. As soon as I arrived there, I realized what was going on. The old man – not for the first time – had fallen in love. She was a very young and beautiful Greek lady, a lady who had also just arrived in Palm Beach for her ... honeymoon. Her new husband was an extremely rich Greek industrialist who looked like the twin of King Farouk of Egypt. He was very fat, quite bald and wore thick glasses. He was also much older than his bride. Her parents had thought it a good match for their daughter, but by the time the marriage had been arranged, she had met and fallen for my old man. My mother, a saint if ever there was one, looked away, as was her custom. So I became the beard. The trouble was that Farouk II, as I shall call that poor man, encouraged his wife to spend her time with old Dad rather than with me, because she and I had too much in common where age and tastes were concerned. (Farouk II did not swim or go dancing.)

My old man had bought a Thunderbird in Palm Beach, a black convertible job, and one of the very first T-birds to go on the market. In that splendid vehicle, I drove Farouk II around, showing him the sights, while his bride and my Daddy remained back at the hotel. I had made a friend while down there named Sean Flynn, son of Errol, the legendary rogue and film star. Sean got around on a powerful motorcycle and disparaged my T-bird, calling it 'an old lady's car'. We had decided to settle our differences once and for all on New Year's Eve, when the police would be kept busy ferrying rich drunks back to their villas and hotels.

On the last night of the year, we all went to the Everglades Club, an exclusive country club on Worth Avenue, for its traditional dinner-dance. Sean and I got rather plastered and after 4 a.m., when the grown-ups had returned to the Breakers Hotel, we lined up our machines and drag-raced all over the club's golf course. Sean beat me easily.

The first sight my eyes met the next morning was the stetson hat of an extremely stern-looking state trooper who roused me out of bed and literally frogmarched me out of the hotel and down to the police station. Sean was already there. It seems the damage we had caused to the club's greens was in the vicinity of thirty thousand big ones, and some very angry members were now demanding our heads. We both admitted our guilt and were locked up for the morning. Sean's mother, Lily Damita, a long-time resident of Palm Beach, arrived after lunch and bailed him out. My time came soon after.

Needless to say, the club was insured and the powers that be did not choose to press charges. When one is the son of a film star or of a Greek shipowner, people are less eager to see justice done than they are, say, if a poor Mexican throws a stone through the window of a Hollywood biggie. So, for us, matters were settled most amicably and I returned to school a hero of sorts for having pulled a number on the club and for having spent a half-day in jail.

Sean and I kept up our friendship and years later we drove together from Paris to St Tropez to 'hunt for women', as Byron used to put it. By the time I got to Vietnam in 1971 he was already dead, having driven his bike through a checkpoint outside Phnom Penh in Cambodia in the company of Dana Stone, while tripping on acid. Sean was terribly attractive to the fair sex, a pretty good athlete, intelligent and at times very sweet as a friend, but strangely tortured and insecure. To say he had a death wish would be a gross understatement. Apparently the Cambodian Commies didn't even waste a bullet on him but simply chopped off his head.

My first New Year's present comes from my landing officer, his assurance that I shall stay on in my cell alone. I tell him that, if I do, he shall go to heaven, and he gives me a great big smile. Frank Heavy, the officer in the gym, arrives after breakfast and gives me my next present, a couple of sandwiches and a pie from his wife. Heavy is a hell of a screw, polite and fatherly to everyone, but firm when it comes to the rules. Except for today. Although he's not supposed to feed the animals, he tells me to admit who gave me the goodies, should I get caught. He also says that he will try like hell to keep the gym job open for me, in case I get my problems straightened out. If anyone will end up in heaven, it's Frank Heavy.

As there is no exercise period I pace up and down the cell, but my heart isn't in it. Finally I stop and sit down and begin to reread *Appointment in Samarra*, a book that had impressed me greatly when I first read it as an eighteen-year-old. Now I find O'Hara slightly dated, even a bit juvenile. But I like the hero, Julian English, and compare him to myself as we both got off on the right foot and ended up deep in the shit. Pretty soon my thoughts drift back to the good old days, and once again to Sean Flynn. Both he and I had clearly set up a collision course in our lives; yet, I think, we both had also set ourselves the highest standards. Sean had openly admitted to having set such standards, and perhaps they were the reason he took such enormous chances with his life. I, on the other hand, would certainly never admit to setting any standards of any kind, but secretly I had. And secretly I knew it. But I was simply too terrified at not being able to meet them. That fear, coupled with my absolute love of human pleasure, made sure I kept on bargaining with myself. 'Well, just a little longer, and then I'll . . .'

Perhaps this prison spell will finally do the trick.

But I doubt it.

· *2 January 1985* ·

Mr Scott is a nice screw who has asked me to give him the stamps from the letters I've been receiving. Some of them come from deepest Africa, where kind *Spectator* readers, having read of my predicament, write encouraging epistles. I like Mr Scott because he's fair with everyone and doesn't give the impression that he thinks we're dirt. The first letter I open is from Arnaud de Borchgrave, the man who got me to enter the business of journalism in 1967. Arnaud has now left *Newsweek* and is travelling around giving speeches to the converted. Known as 'the last foreign correspondent of the trench-coat school', he has covered more wars and disasters than anyone, interviewed more big shots than a gossip columnist, travelled more widely than a cosmonaut and is a hell of a good friend. Although I've already mentioned him in the Preface, my travails with Arnaud are worth a closer look, if only because they're so amusing. A bit like Inspector Clouseau taking up the journalistic profession.

I took my first trip with him just about the time he was breaking new ground by interviewing Nasser in Cairo, and then crossing the Allenby Bridge to chat with Golda Meir. It made the front pages all over the world, and I, as his assistant and special photographer, basked in his glory.

But there was trouble. Arnaud has been described as 'a

walking ulcer' because of his unrestrained energy, his constant need, bordering on the manic, to keep busy. While I,
to use a euphemism of sorts, like to relax. While Arnaud
paced the room, worrying whether some head of state
would call or not, I would flop out on the bed or sofa and
read my books on Napoleon. This would enrage him
almost as much as when I would refuse to get out of bed
in the morning, a useless exercise, as I had – shall we say?
– very little to do. So he devised a scheme to make me
responsible. Whenever we would be in some hot spot of
the world, say Cairo, he would order me to go out at once
and photograph local colour, as well as things like bridges,
army barracks and tank depots. 'Get the picture, get the
picture!' he would yell at me – very early in the morning.

Which, in Cairo, I tried to do.

But no sooner had I snapped the shutter than a howling
Arab mob came after me, screaming that I was an Israeli
spy. Having seen what Arabs do to a fellow when they
outnumber him two hundred to one, I ran straight for a
police station and demanded to be arrested. But not before
about ten of those towel-heads had punched me around
and broken the camera. Arnaud's reaction was typical.
'You mean you didn't get any pictures?'

Yet 'the short count', as Arnaud is affectionately known
in the trade, thanks to his physical stature and title, did
introduce me to his contacts and show me the ropes.
Among them was the pretty wife of a famous French
journalist, a photographer of note in her own right
who specialized in the Middle East. For obvious reasons,
I will not reveal her name. In 1970, when King Hussein
threw out the PLO from Amman in a bloody ten-day
war, I happened to be in Beirut, reporting for the
National Review. Mrs X, as I shall call her, was also there,
trying to get to Amman, as were the rest of the hacks

overrunning the St George Hotel. I had hitched up with two *Paris Match* photographers, Allen Tayeb and Jean-Pierre Boscardo, both old Vietnam hands who knew their way around. We decided to drive to Amman, as the airport in the capital of Jordan was as hard to fly into as Pentonville is to get out of. Mrs X thought our plan foolhardy, but nevertheless entrusted me with a personal letter for King Hussein.

Well, that was one epistle that went astray. Once out of Irbid, in the north of Jordan, we were intercepted by a Palestinian column of fighters whose mood was not exactly friendly. Their brothers-in-arms were getting the hell knocked out of them by the King's Arab Legion, and in such situations the losing side tends to get rather nasty. They locked us up in a room, posted an armed guard outside, and told us to say our prayers. Tayeb and Boscardo remained cool and collected, but I was a bit more worried. William F. Buckley's organ wasn't exactly pro-Palestinian, so I figured my days of driving over greens of chic country clubs had come to an untimely end.

And there was also the problem with the letter.

Being a curious type, I opened it and read it. It was the closest thing to hard-core pornography I had ever come across, so graphic in its details of the King's anatomy and what Mrs X would like to do with certain parts of it that for an instant I forgot about my predicament and got excited.

My two buddies read it also and immediately demanded that I eat it. As they put it, 'If they find this, we won't even get a decent burial.' So the three of us sat right down and made a meal of the letter, swallowing the last bite just as a ferocious-looking sort came in and began grilling us. Soon, however, we were allowed to go free, as long as we headed back towards Lebanon, a place that, ironic as it may sound today, was as safe as anywhere in the Middle East. Once back in Beirut I looked for Mrs X, but she had returned to Paris. I never saw her again, and thus never told her where her letter had ended up. While sitting in my cell this morning and thinking back, I cannot help but conclude that carrying envelopes is no good for me.

Although a close call, my little encounter with the pride of Palestine paled by comparison to my next one, three years later, this time on the Israeli side. By then I was reporting for a Greek daily, *Acropolis*, and was in Tel Aviv covering the Yom Kippur War of October 1973. Tayeb and Boscardo weren't around, so I hitched up with Joe Fried, back, then, with New York's *Daily News*, Jean-Claude Sauer, an old friend with *Paris Match*, and the most unlikely foreign correspondent down there, ex-Group Captain Peter Townsend, the Battle of Britain hero and former suitor of Princess Margaret. Despite the fact that he had shot down countless German fighter planes, Townsend had never seen a dead man before and he was green, to say the least, as to how one goes about the front. Fried was the most experienced, then came Sauer. The trouble was that Jean-Claude had brought a friend along, one Alix Chevassus, a French playboy of some repute and the man who married the Greek shipping heiress Maria Niarchos for one month. Sauer had been sitting in Régine's, in Paris when the call came to fly down to Israel and, as he was rather drunk, had invited Alix, drinking next to him, to come along for the ride.

I had rented a car and the five of us piled in every morning and drove up towards Al-Kuneitra on the Golan Heights, where furious tank battles were taking place. Sauer, an ex-racing driver, had been entrusted with the driving and, until the particular day I have in mind, did an excellent job. Driving around the front is always a tricky business because the trucks ferrying back the damaged goods simply do not obey normal traffic laws. If you are in the way, they will simply run over you. There were also some ambulances racing around, bringing back the wounded, so I cautioned Jean-Claude repeatedly to slow down. Needless to say, he did nothing of the sort. In fact, Alix the playboy gave me the distinct impression that he was enjoying himself. Later, he annoyed me no end by asking me why I was so afraid of speed. But just as his question came, a rocket exploded next to the car, sending us scrambling out to take cover. Everyone but Alix, that is, who had frozen with fear and was unable to move a muscle.

I ran a zig-zag course for about fifty yards, doing what I had seen countless actors do in war films, which was – as I soon found out – not exactly the smartest way to survive because I was running in a minefield. Once Fried informed me of this, I did 'an Alix' and remained motionless, fixed in a prone position. Sauer was screaming for me to get Alix out – I was closer to him – as 'we'll never be allowed back into Régine's again if we lose him!' Then someone had the bright idea of telling Alix that heat-seeking missiles were sure to home straight in on the car he was sitting in, and, of course, that little titbit did the trick. Alix was out and in no time resembling Jesse Owens. The little jet-set drama had a happy ending when an Israeli platoon trundled by and helped guide me out of my predicament with their mine-detectors.

After that farcical episode, I decided to stick close to Joe Fried, an experienced hand, as cynical and hard-boiled as he was generous with his advice. Joe is a small, wiry man, from Brooklyn I believe, with a heavy 'Noo Yawk' accent and an aggressive manner to match. There are stories galore about his antics at the '5 o'clock follies', as the daily Vietnam press briefings were known in Saigon. One of the best stories making the rounds about him is surely apocryphal but worth repeating. Apparently, Ruth Fried, Joe's wife, had arrived in Saigon to meet him after a very long separation. It was her first visit to that unhappy land and in typical Jewish-wife manner she began to harangue Joe while he was driving her from Than Son Nhut airport to the city. 'Joe, what is this, what kind of dump is this, Joe?' she kept repeating. Once inside their flat, she took a look around the place and continued to bitch. 'Joe, there's no air-condition, how do you expect me to live in this dump without air-condition, Joe?'

Fried had already sat down at his typewriter and was blazing away when a rocket crashed through their roof, without exploding because of the flimsiness of the house. While Ruth threw herself underneath a sofa, Joe never missed a beat. He kept on typing, but looked up and yelled at her, 'Are you happy now, Ruthie, now you've got air-condition?'

The second letter is from Maria St Just, Gore Vidal and Sue Mengers in Venice. The last time I saw Gore, it was at Maria's grand country house and he was in excellent form. 'Poor you,' he told me. 'They were looking for me or Jerry Brown and instead they landed a small right-wing fish like you.' Vidal's theories about right-wing conspiracies are as ludicrous as his politics, but he's a wonderful man and wonderful company. Like all good artists, he is unstinting with his advice and encouraging to those who don't possess his talent. Sue Mengers I don't know well, but I am moved by her kind letter, especially in view of my often published opinions of Hollywood and the supremely unsympathetic gallery of hustlers, sub-Runyonesque crooks, creeps and showbiz schmucks that inhabit the place.

Countless books and films have told of the ghastliness of the place, its false values and wrong priorities, yet Hollywood goes on unperturbed, the leader of the pack, so to speak, advertising itself shamelessly and consistently. Yes, if in a thousand years' time sociologists and anthropologists unearth the reasons for Western culture having taken a nosedive somewhere during the second half of the twentieth century, Hollywood will finally receive the historical and cultural recognition it well deserves. But today what I hate most about Hollywood is the way it fell into line with the kind of anti-Americanism practised by the media during the sixties, a line that Hollywood continues to toe well into the eighties, while remaining oblivious to mainstream American thinking. The line I am talking about is that inexplicable, quasi-intellectual, vindictive view of Uncle Sam propagated by the Noam Chomskys, Abbie Hoffmans and Tom Fondas of this world. The line that portrays most military men as sadists and bloodthirsty killers, priests as charlatans and sexual perverts, small-town dwellers as red-necked bigots and businessmen as total crooks.

Why does Hollywood choose to remain so removed from reality? Search me, I don't know. What I do know is that, in the old days, the tycoons who ran the place may have believed culture to be a piano-shaped swimming pool, but they appreciated the artistic and personal freedom America provided and they showed their appreciation in their films. Most of these hotshots had come from East European ghettos; they had first-hand knowledge of bigotry and what it meant to be a third-rate citizen. I only wish some of our present-day tycoons would uproot themselves and live under the benevolent rule of Soviet Russia, and compare.

*

This afternoon I am reminded of the Hollywood double standard while I work away next to Warren, listening to him excoriate Margaret Thatcher. According to Warren, Hitler and Stalin were benevolent leaders compared to Mrs T. I suppose that listening to such bullshit is better than being completely deaf, but I'm not sure. I try and change Warren's mind, although he's as likely to believe me as I am to believe his ideology. Somewhere along the line, I guess, the grandiose rhetoric of our political leaders had the opposite effect of the one they'd intended. They promised to make men into gods, their countries into Utopia, and those who took them at their word now see our society as rotten to the core. Warren should live among his Caribbean brothers to see what real poverty is like. Even while he's in jail, his family is being taken care of by the state, the very state Warren hates with such a passion.

· 3 January 1985 ·

Two West Indians have been screaming abuse at everything and everyone throughout the night. I can tell they're
Rastafarians by the racist tone of the abuse they're heaping
out. Two whites, meanwhile, are giving it back to them in
spades, no pun intended. The shouting lasts almost until
dawn and by the time they become too exhausted to go
on, I've picked up a large new vocabulary of racial insults.

No screws ever come to the aid of those who want to
sleep. Once we're locked in for the night, no screw will
venture inside the cells. Occasionally we hear the judas
hole clank as the warders check, but unless there is a
break no warder ever opens up, no matter what the com-
plaint. Many stories are making the rounds, stories of prisoners who set fire to their mattresses and die from smoke
inhalation while their screams go unanswered.

On my way down to breakfast I hear more details about
the American drug dealer who hanged himself in the
remand wing last week. Prisoners waiting to be tried have
the right to keep their personal clothes, and the American
hanged himself with his belt. The scuttlebutt is that he was
facing a very long stretch, forty years, and took the easy
way out. Pavlo, my Cypriot friend who is also a drug
dealer and a master of cliché, says that the man was dumb.
'Where there's life, there's hope.'

*

Being a prisoner myself, I cannot exactly feel elated that one more dealer is dead, but I find very little sympathy for his species. Mind you, it's people like me who keep them in their rotten business, people like me and rock stars, as well as the movie crowd, Wall Street, etc., etc. In fact, I remember a 1971 *Rolling Stone* interview in which John Lennon bragged about how he'd taken 'a thousand LSD trips, and used to eat it all the time'. In a 1967 *Life* article, Paul McCartney called LSD a 'cure-all'. Many other celebrities not only agreed but proselytized; as a result, a considerable number of urban children cheerfully took a proffered joint or a sniff ... Why refuse when it was something Mick Jagger or John Lennon had used and enjoyed?

The greatest irony of the drug culture was that the period at its peak was called 'the era of love'. In reality, the sixties were among the most hate-filled and violent times in American history. It was also the best time self-indulgent students ever had. Although, as purported, a great debate may have been going on about the nature of society and radical political possibilities, those speeches always seemed to me ill-thought-out, self-serving and abusive. I did not touch drugs then and each day my frustration rose to new heights as questions about the failure of capitalism were answered with references to the shining example of Mao's China, then, in fact, being torn apart by the worst excesses of the Cultural Revolution. The protesters, while claiming to be altruists, were really seeking to destroy academic authority. Students who had voluntarily put themselves under the extremely mild discipline of American universities were now behaving as though they suffered the whips of the Gestapo or, better yet, of Chinese Red Guards.

If the campus radicals of the sixties were looking for

genuine change, they were cowards in choosing the university as their first object of attack. After all, the university stands as one of the sole pockets of reason where change remains possible through non-violent means. Real revolutionaries blow up power stations, assassinate political leaders, derail trains and take to the streets. They do not hide behind the skirts of a college administration and then, unwilling to accept the consequences of their actions, demand amnesty. After all, what risk is involved in roughing up some paunchy dean? Radical student self-glorification rose to its zenith in Paris in 1968, just as Russian tanks rolled into Prague and showed the world how real power carries on.

I had spent most of the spring of that year in Paris, playing polo by day and by night watching the student riots from the safety of Régine's on the Boulevard Montparnasse, where the 'Queen of the Night' was then located. In May, when things began to get hot literally as well as metaphorically, the polo powers decided to cancel the season. I was furious because of the humbug involved. The Paris riots of 1968 had begun when a lot of middle-class students revolted against the middle-class morality of their parents. For a lot of middle-class French polo enthusiasts to panic and give in was to me the height of hypocrisy. After all, we continued to play practice matches, and the French bourgeoisie continued to weekend in their country houses, eat their sumptuous meals and see their mistresses even more regularly as there was more time in view of the strikes, so why cancel a noble sport played mostly by Argentines, although paid for by the French?

While some of us were threatening to take our horses and go to England, a tragedy occurred that put a damper on polo for the year. Elie de Rothschild, a leading member of French polo and a scion of the banking family, was struck by a ball during a particularly lively practice match and lost his eye. While he lay in hospital, a bunch of so-called Maoists tried to invade the club. I was very happy to lead a polo charge, patterned after the Cossack charge in the film of *Dr Zhivago*. The response of the club was instant. I was suspended indefinitely. Needless to say, no one had been hurt because the Maoists saw us from afar and beat the hastiest retreat in history, but the club feared that the publicity would be appalling if the story ever got out. It did not, and Elie de Rothschild, to his credit, lifted the suspension as soon as he left the hospital.

1968 was a pretty bad year. Cristina and I had broken up that spring, the Tet offensive had sapped morale back in the States, Paris was in turmoil, I was desperate for a job in journalism and I even managed to get Régine's attacked by the dreaded French riot police, the CRS.

Unlike her various clubs of today, Régine's at that time was small and dark, an intimate place known for its lack of air-conditioning and its great atmosphere. It was called 'New Jimmy's' and it was packed every night, especially during '*Les Événements*', because, unlike other club owners, Régine refused to be intimidated by the rioters and kept her place open. In fact, she went further than that; she openly advertised that she was against the students and for de Gaulle.

For those who lived on the Boulevards Raspail and Montparnasse, the nightly street battles were great theatre. I had many a dinner *chez* Régine, upstairs in her flat where, after dining and before descending to the club below, we would watch the shenanigans. Régine always had a soft spot in her heart for me, perhaps because Rubirosa and I were among her first good clients or perhaps because of the time I returned from playing Davis Cup in Ireland, found out that Cristina (then nineteen years old) was out dancing, and stormed into Régine's place looking for a fight. I did catch Cristina *in flagrante*, teaching the twist to the Duke of Windsor, and Régine has dined out on the story ever since.

On this particular night, however, I had other plans. Plans involving a young Brazilian girl who was studying in Paris and was passionately on the side of the students. She and I dined on the Right Bank and argued throughout over the obvious. Gidgy was extremely attractive, but she irritated me beyond belief by insisting on the unfairness of the 'system' and of capitalism in general. But the idea that, even as we were talking, Soviet tanks were actually poised to go in against students in Prague who were in revolt to demand the privileges their French counterparts were complaining about outraged me. My point was that, as long as one's civil rights were upheld by the courts, there was no call for civil disobedience.

After dinner, I insisted she have a drink at Régine's and we drove over the bridge and on towards 'New Jimmy's'. On the way, as luck would have it, we ran into a large demonstration and students soliciting funds '*Pour la Révolution*' stopped us. Well, after so many years it is easy to distort the truth, but the fact is that I simply could not lose face in front of such a beautiful girl. So I stopped trembling and dramatically announced that they could kill me if they liked, but I was against them and therefore I refused. Some of the students began to rock the car, but almost immediately a man with an armband came over and politely asked me to go on.

Once outside Régine's, I sent Gidgy inside and remained where I was, watching the pitched battle that was raging a quarter-mile down the street, directly in front of Papa Hemingway's old haunt, 'La Clôserie des Lilas'. Suddenly the black-garbed CRS charged in unison. The students broke and ran. And, just as suddenly, I found myself in the middle and knocked on Régine's door, which opened to let me in. Unfortunately, others had the same idea. While Régine and her waiters tried desperately to stop the students from entering, the riot police arrived, mistook the place as one of pro-student sympathies, and fired a long volley of tear-gas grenades into it.

You can imagine the rest.

Under ideal circumstances the club was hard to breathe in, but filled with tear gas it became Dante's Inferno. At best the jet-set tends to panic easily, and that night it broke all records. Once outside, the various playboys and their bimbos met an even nastier surprise. The CRS are all to a man drawn from the provinces. They did not recognize some of the most illustrious members of '*tout Paris*', but instead went to work on them. Régine banned me for a week, but wrote about the incident in her autobiography. Frankly, I was rather proud of the whole affair.

Almost as proud as I feel when suddenly an officer comes down to the workshop and tells me to go up and see the assistant governor right away. In prison, whenever one is called by the governor, more often than not it means bad news. A death in the family, an appeal turned down, a punishment to be meted out. But this is my lucky day. The assistant 'gov' is a small man with bad skin and an arrogant manner but, after he tells me, I could almost kiss him. 'You must have friends in high places,' is the way he puts it, 'because your appeal to be reinstated as a C-prisoner has gone through in record time.' (I did have Lord Goodman write to the Home Office, the head of which is a regular *Spectator* reader, as are all the cabinet.) Which means I can have my old job back, which makes me happier than anything I can remember in years.

It is an old custom among inmates not to show great joy when something good happens in order not to rub it in to the others. Some do and it looks awful. I think of this as I go back to pick up my denim jacket and hand in my tools. I tell Warren and the other Rastas working next to me that they should come to the gym where I'll take good care of them, say goodbye to the rest, but make it a point to ignore the white-jacketed supervisor who has never heard of Oscar Wilde.

Frank Heavy and Mr Leggett and Andy Gordon welcome me with smiles all round and inform me with winks and nods that they were about to take someone else on. Who said that one cannot be happy in prison?

· 4 January 1985 ·

Good things come in twos. After breakfast Mr Scott opens
my door and informs me that the last cell on the landing's
end has just been vacated. Would I be interested? Is the
Pope interested in prayer? The end cell in every landing
contains only one bed and is reserved for troublemakers
who can't get along with their cellmates. Single occupancy
is considered a punishment in prison. Almost as important, however, is the fact that the single cell is located next
to the single toilet of the landing, which means that the
occupant has a hell of an advantage when it comes to the
slop-out dash.

The numbing monotony of prison life aside, it's the
unsanitary conditions that breed trouble in jail. Prisoners
frequently have to paddle through other men's urine
towards the end of the slopping-out session, as the drains
cannot cope with the volume of use. Getting there before
everyone is probably the single greatest advantage one can
enjoy in the nick. I contemplate my good fortune as I pack
my few belongings and steel myself for the mess I am
bound to find waiting for me in cell 36, D-4, my final
destination until F-day I hope.

The only shower facilities in Pentonville are in the gym.
The rest of the fifteen-hundred-odd prisoners have to make
do with the ten or fifteen bathtubs next to the laundry.
Inmates are herded there once a week for a bath and a

change of sheet. I say 'sheet' because, although one is issued two sheets upon arrival, one sheet is all a prisoner gets to exchange per week. Bathing in prison, needless to say, is not exactly like bathing in Marienbad. During the week I was sewing army uniforms, I almost had a taste of it, but for reasons known only to myself I chose to ignore the privilege. I was waiting in line while the men in front of me took five minutes each to run a bath and plunge in. The two men immediately preceding me decided to luxuriate a bit longer, so they dispensed with the running of the bath and waded right into the grimy water, not bothering to empty the tub. When my turn came, I gave it a pass, deciding right there and then that I would go without a bath for the duration. But now all this seems long ago.

After dinner, about 2 p.m., I get permission from Mr Wrigley to go down to D-1 and do some business with Sid's replacement, a pretty good sort I am told. (Landing orderlies are picked by the officer in charge, and are the cream of the crop.) I offer tobacco in exchange for disinfectant, and cigarettes in return for a brand-new mop. I spend the rest of the day spraying antiseptic all over my cell and scrubbing away with the cleanest mop this side of the Carlyle Hotel.

· *5 January 1985* ·

For someone who got rid of the most beautiful sailing boat in the world because it was too slow and confining, I now find that the 13′ by 7′ world of D-4-36 seems to suit me to a T. I feel happy and safe, and still cannot get over my good luck in having a single cell, and a clean mop to boot. Not to mention my job in the gym. Once again I feel that I have gone to the brink and emerged unscathed. I guess that ineluctable collision course with fate has not taken place. Or, if it has, I've sailed through it as I've sailed through everything else in life.

Doing time gives one the opportunity to think about such weighty subjects as one's direction in life, but this morning *gravitas* must be avoided at all costs. Being Greek, I'm very superstitious, and fully aware of hubris's consequences. If I have escaped yet again, the last thing I wish to do is remind the gods of it. Having had the slightest of tastes of what it takes to be kicked into maturity, I decide to do a Scarlett O'Hara and leave the introspection for another day. For the moment, I am content to lie in bed, waiting for the knock on my door while I contemplate happiness. For me it means my good job, my clean cell and my privacy. Everything I had on the outside and threw away.

Today is also my first visiting day. I asked the editor of

the *Spectator*, Charles Moore, and another close friend, Oliver Gilmour, and both returned the slip, indicating they will be coming. Each prisoner is allowed one visiting day every twenty-eight days. Visits entail the following: a guard comes to the workplace of the inmate and escorts him to an ante-room where the prisoner is searched before he is taken into a large square room that serves as a cafeteria/visiting hall. There is a small canteen where visitors are allowed to purchase chocolate and soft drinks. Nothing more. The visit lasts approximately half an hour.

Charles and Oliver both went to Eton, but didn't know each other before I introduced them. Charles, as the youngest editor of the *Spectator*, looks older than his twenty-eight years, while Oliver, who is thirty-one, acts younger. He is a conductor, a serious classical music student and the son of Sir Ian Gilmour, the long-time Tory member of parliament and minister in various Conservative governments. Ollie is a hell-raiser and a drinker. Charles is almost too well behaved. They are already sitting down and waiting for me as I'm led in and they greet me as if we're at Annabel's. I notice that their upper-class demeanour and accent have already drawn the attention of the screws, which I have been told is not a good sign. Charles tells me that a lot of mail has come from readers voicing their support and that my job is secure as long as I do not repeat my little envelope trick. Oliver says that the bar at Annabel's is not the same without me, and that the staff of the club are the ones who ask about me the most. It does not surprise me, as they are by far the nicest people in the joint.

But there is no use kidding myself. I am deeply embarrassed to be sitting down with Charles and Oliver under such circumstances, and my conversation shows it. Mercifully, the screws break it up earlier than they're supposed to, and I quickly shake hands with my friends and am taken away. Then I am searched very thoroughly and escorted back to work.

Back in the gym again, I realized that neither of my two friends asked me what it is like to be in jail. I guess this is 'Britishness' at its best. Stiff upper lip and all that. Or perhaps they thought I might not know the code and complain. But a swift depression descends upon me as a result of the visit, which served to remind me of how pleasant life is on the outside and the enormity of my self-indulgence when I had access to it.

This afternoon I train extra hard trying to take my mind off the morning's thoughts, but then a strange thing happens. For the first time since coming to Pentonville, I start thinking of sex. Pornographers like Larry Flint will obviously not agree, but prison proves beyond any reasonable doubt that the baser instincts of man can be kept within bounds if he's deprived of pornography. The proof is in the porridge. I have thought of sex every day of my life ever since I discovered what it was, but here I am, close to three weeks without seeing a woman, and I have yet to think of carnal matters. A lifelong sensualist, cured of my chronic yearnings in less than a month! How wonderful it would be if my prison experience inspired me, by my own example, to discover a universal truth! (A frequently broadcast truth, to be sure, but from what mouths? The fork-tongued mouths of liberals, bleeding-hearts, feminists?) Or does the answer lie elsewhere? After all, so much of prison life is made up of the most elemental struggle to survive. And, for the survivor, surviving with deprivation from all sides, one's own insides to begin with. I suppose one might better make a case for fear and starvation as the cure for sexual appetite.

But humankind is infinitely adaptable. Given sufficient time, no pun intended, I might feel physically safer and better accustomed to prison fare and the whole barrel of old sexual urges would no doubt turn upside down in one sudden split-second and flood me with longing.

If it does, though, I like to believe that my own mind and its talent at invention would provide the details. Not the obscene videos, not the porn flicks, not the skin magazines. Take away the whole shebang and you take away far less sexuality than outright violence. In short, remove the pornography and you might also remove the nastiest commercial inducements to rape women and to behave violently towards them. Not to mention child-molestation. Man's instincts are perverse enough. Do we really need a market aimed at encouraging them at their worst?

I find nothing more repulsive than the sex barons. But I hold in almost as much contempt those literary highbrows who boost the mammoth profits of the porn kings by piously declaring that a civilized society cannot have censorship of any sort. That's as big a cop-out as blaming America for Third World ills. Feminists should go after the intelligentsia backing such rubbish with the same vigour they go after male chauvinist pigs like me.

And speaking of sex, I found myself staring at a young inmate's legs this afternoon – an inmate, mind you, who looked highly effeminate. It reminded me of boarding-school, when one would look at another boy in the showers, but didn't want to know why. Thank God my sentence is short because, sooner or later, even the most heterosexual of species will turn towards its own if deprived of the opposite sex. Warren says that in English prisons sex is easier to find than on the outside. There are male prostitutes whose protectors rent them out. I've seen nothing of it in Pentonville, however, because everyone is locked up most of the time. I guess that is what cellmates are for.

When the young prisoner I caught myself looking at comes to pick up his shorts and jersey, I almost throw them at him. Then I remember D. H. Lawrence's short story about a Prussian officer and give him a smile.

· *6 January 1985* ·

I have settled down to a routine of hard exercise and weightlifting. Thirty minutes of stretching, followed by weights for forty-five. After that I skip rope for ten minutes, take a shower, sweep the gym, collect the dirty clothes, take them to the laundry and then eat dinner and get locked up. All this by 11.45 in the morning. The afternoon session begins at 1.30 p.m. when I once again hand out shorts, training shoes and jerseys, and then exercise on my own. I hit the heavy bag for five three-minute rounds, do my karate kicks and punches in the air for speed, and finish with more stretching. Then I collect the dirty clothes, take a shower and have tea in my cell. When everybody else gets locked up for the night, I go back to the gym, where a different landing has an exercise period six times per week. More often than not, I join in a basketball game or indoor soccer, both of which are played very aggressively by the inmates, although the quality is as low as one can find anywhere. Criminals are not exactly natural athletes, at least none of the ones I've met. With the exception of Trevor Middleton.

Trevor is a tall, good-looking black man of about twenty-five, who looks like Muhammad Ali did at that age. Trevor is the only man I've seen jump a badminton net without a running leap. He simply stands about a foot away, bends his knees and gives a mighty leap. He's in for

violent assault on a policeman who, Trevor claims, tried
to rape his girlfriend. When he told me the story I started
to laugh because Trevor doesn't look like the type whose
girlfriend might get raped. 'Were you present when he
tried it?' I asked him.

'Yeah, man, that's why I bashed him up,' came the
answer. With a wink and a nod and a very loud laugh.

Not knowing many black people on the outside, I find it
ironic that my three closest friends in prison are all black –
Warren, Trevor and Lee Anderson, a Jamaican with whom
I kick-box twice a week in the gym. Anderson is a tough
customer and I try to stay away from him as he likes to
mix it. He's stronger than I am, but I've got experience,
something he has yet to acquire. Anderson, too, is a
natural athlete, and this evening he tries something on me
that no one has yet. He walks on his hands and attacks
with his feet, a useless exercise because all I do is push him
off. The trouble is, as he falls, he wrenches his shoulder
out of its socket and ends up in great pain writhing on the
floor. The rules about injury in prison are simple. No one
is allowed to take the prisoner to the hospital unless a
male nurse and two guards are present. One also needs
permission from a doctor to go to the hospital, located
across the yard.

While Lee lies helpless on the floor, Frank Heavy tries
to ring for the doctor, but without success. I am finally
forced to leave Lee back in the gym when the class is over.
I find out later from Frank that it took two hours for the
medic to arrive.

· *7 January 1985* ·

While I wait in line for chow this morning, Roger, the librarian, tells me he's reading *Past Imperfect*, Joan Collins's autobiography, and there's a character called Taki in it. It kills me to deny its real-life inspiration, but deny it I do. What is the use of impressing a poor librarian jailbird, and one who's gay, to boot?

I first heard I had been included in her – shall we say steamy? – memoirs when Peregrine Worsthorne, the patrician columnist of the *Sunday Telegraph*, told me about it over lunch one day. For somebody as serious as Perry, he seemed awfully impressed. I wonder what it is about celebrities that makes even weighty men turn groupie.

La Collins wrote her opus in the late seventies, just before she struck it rich with *Dynasty*. It doesn't exactly have the depth and style of, say, Benjamin Franklin's autobiography, but it's better than the crap her sister churns out. The title alone is worth the price of the book (as Ilka Chase's readers must also have thought in 1947 when *her* book of memoirs, *Past Imperfect*, first came out). Although I disapprove of men spilling the beans about the ladies they've bedded, such behaviour in reverse doesn't bother me a bit. (Is my sexism showing again? If so, I wonder what it's saying.) In any case, I was flattered to be included in Collins's list of 'past imperfections'.

Joan and I met in 1957, when I was twenty years old

and she a bit older. It was, as they say, love at first sight and I forgot all about my tennis while I pursued her from New York to Los Angeles. My schedule back then was simple. I woke up with a hangover, went over to a tennis club and hit tennis balls until dark. I then picked up whomever I was picking up and went out to dinner and a nightclub. One day a sudden downpour flooded the courts, so I returned early to the Sherry-Netherland Hotel where I lived. On the way in, I passed the restaurant and noticed Joan lunching with my father. I thought it rather odd, as my father never had lunch but used the time to go to his club and have a steam bath, but what was even odder was the diamond pin Joan was wearing. It was an anchor, I believe. Twenty-five years later, while reading her book, I got the message. One that I cannot go into in detail, except to say that you'll find more beautiful women walking around in Athens wearing jewels with a maritime theme than you'll find name-droppers in Hollywood. No wonder the old man looked ill at ease that day.

One year later, Joan having gone on to bigger and better things, another sudden downpour caused further embarrassment. It was the time I was running around with Linda Christian (yes, she too has written her memoirs and spilled the beans), and she and I were living at the Sherry-Netherland, where I had persuaded the manager to allow me to stay in my father's apartment. I was following my usual schedule and while I trained, Linda shopped or lunched with friends.

As luck would have it, the torrential rains came early in the fateful day and I was back at the Sherry by 11 a.m. Not in my apartment, however. Someone had locked the door from the inside and no amount of ringing brought any response. So I went looking for the engineer. I found him almost immediately. But just as he was about to tackle the stubborn door, it opened and out stepped a small, bald man wearing thick-rimmed glasses and an aggressive look on his face. To my challenge of 'What the hell are you doing in my apartment?', he drew himself up to his full height of approximately five feet and announced that he was the godfather of Linda's children and how dare I speak to him this way! If memory serves, I think I asked him how come he was godfather to both children, and then to identify himself. 'My name is McConnell,' he said loud and clear and quickly side-stepped me and disappeared down the hall.

Once inside, I found Linda lounging on the bed smoking a cigarette. When I confronted her with being behind locked doors with a bald, myopic midget she merely laughed. 'But that's McConnell, the godfather of Romina.' Naïve boy that I was, I let it drop.

That evening, on my way out, the doorman at the Sherry, a very nice Cuban man who knew me well, joked about what I had done to Mr Lazar. When I told him that I knew no Mr Lazar, he described McConnell. I quickly got the message. I'd had my first meeting with Swifty Lazar, *agent extraordinaire*, and obviously a man who knew how to extricate himself from sticky situations. (He'd had a quickie with Linda and, when I stopped him outside, had yelled his name of the moment at me so she would hear it. Humphrey Bogart was right to have named him 'Swifty'. A quick thinker Irving Lazar sure is.)

The next time I spoke with Swifty was exactly twenty-three years later, at a grand English ball in the country. Before that, I had often made fun of him in print and, seated across from him at the ball, I was expecting the worst. But he was all sweetness and light. 'I don't mind what you write, kid,' he said. 'Most people think I'm a legend. It's good you bring me down a peg or two.'

Legend or not, only Hollywood could have invented Swifty Lazar, if he didn't exist.

· 8 January 1985 ·

A long day in the gym. I pump a lot of iron and skip rope like mad, do my karate exercises but miss Lee Anderson and the sparring. I also play some badminton, a game that looks easy but is hard to get the knack of, as players need very good reflexes and even better lungs. It is not a sport I've ever been able to get excited about.

After dinner Mr Heavy unlocks me and tells me that there is no gym this evening and challenges me to a prison version of squash. This is played with a paddle tennis racket and a tennis ball, the rules being the same as squash except that the whole length of the gym is used, as well as all natural barriers, such as weights, shower doors and the boxing-bag. (If a player can hit the ball into the shower room or against the bag, he wins the point, etc.) Frank Heavy is excellent at it. In fact, he tells me he's never lost a game in the twenty years he's been in Pentonville. Although he beats me easily, by the third set I'm starting to catch on. The game is certainly a great conditioner and I can't help thinking that, had I followed such a regime while I was a touring tennis player, perhaps my results would not have been as disastrous.

Training in nightclubs for a tennis tournament like the French championships may not be the best way, but it does provide the built-in excuse for failure. Tennis never suited my temperament; above all, the sport requires concentration, a certain lack of imagination and great patience. All sports at top level demand sacrifice, but no sport – with the possible exception of swimming – needs as much from a competitor as tennis. They say that skiing's preparation is as brutal as anything devised by man, and perhaps it is, but the actual racing is over in less than two minutes, thus eliminating concentration as a factor. (Even I can concentrate for that length of time.) Boxing is another sport where the training requirements are egregious, but they have more to do with muscular rather than mental reflexes. And once inside the ring, the die is cast. The fear disappears. The only obstacle remains the opponent. Not in tennis. More often than not, at least in my case, a player beats himself, or plays way below his ability because of the importance of the occasion.

As I said, tennis was a disaster for me. Not only did I not have the temperament to concentrate, I was impatient and, worst of all, played poorly and below par whenever the match was important. Looking back, it is easy to see why. Since tennis was the only thing I did in life, it was imperative that I won, and the more imperative it became, the more I lost. It was a vicious circle, one I got around by finding an excuse for losing – my lifestyle. That the Greek tennis federation briefly saw me as its Great White Hope didn't help, nor did the old man's ironic remarks to his friends that his youngest son had a great future ahead of him in tennis, if only he could beat a ballboy or two. Roy Emerson, the great Australian champion, once told me that he would bet on my beating anyone in the world who spent as much time in nightclubs as I did, and I suppose I could have, but Roy did not mean it as a compliment. He thought my case rather sad, as he liked me a lot and we had some wonderful times together.

During the first round of a doubles match in the French championships at Roland Garros in 1965, my built-in excuse to avoid the truth came to a head. My partner was Nicky Kalogeropoulos, no relation to Maria Kalogeropoulos or to Callas, but an excellent tennis player. In fact, Nicky is the best player ever to play for Greece, although he was born in Costa Rica of a Greek father and learned his tennis down there. Nicky Kalo, as he was known, won both the French and Wimbledon junior championships in 1962, and in later years reached the last sixteen at Wimbledon. He was my doubles partner and we won the Greek national championship in that event many times.

On this day in Paris, during the most important claycourt championship in the world, Nicky and I were playing against Frank Froehling and Cliff Richey, two Americans, both of whom had been ranked in the sixties as number one in the United States. Nicky was playing like a god and for once I, too, was holding up my end. We were leading them by two sets to one, with a chance to serve out the match, when I blew a trick shot (hitting the ball with so much underspin that it bounces back to the side of the court it came from). It cost us the set. And probably the match, which we lost seven games to five in the fifth set. Nicky said nothing to me, but he was disgusted. Cliff Richey and I had words and almost came to blows because he called me names for having tried such a shot. He was later made to apologize by the American Davis Cup captain, but it was too late. Frank Froehling, a good guy, just shook his head. It was obvious to everyone – and we had a hell of a crowd that day on court 13 in Roland Garros – that this was one man who could not face the responsibility of winning. That really was the end for me and I returned to play only the Greek nationals until 1976.

Ironically, having given up tennis, I began to relax, have fun playing the game, and wound up being ranked fourth in Greece at the age of forty.

My only other winning feat in tennis came by accident. While exiled in the Sudan, I entered the Sudanese Open and won it. I was given a gold tray – worth more than most Sudanese earn in their lifetime – which was later stolen from my flat.

Today I follow tennis only during the Wimbledon fortnight. Like most players of my generation, I am appalled at the behaviour and antics of some players today, and amazed at the amount of money the top ones make for playing a fun game in the sun. Whenever I run into some old friends from the circuit, we do what old jocks always tend to do, reminisce, and it's always about some caper I had pulled on court or off. Budge Patty, Fred Stolley, Nicky Pietrangeli, Nicky Pilic, Manuel Santana, Abe Segal, Neale Frazer and Lew Hoad are among those I still see and none of them has ever expressed any bitterness over having just missed the big bucks. In their day tennis was played mostly for glory, a word that is not prevalent in today's climate. The money has changed the nature of the game and, worse, it has changed the nature of the people who play it. I guess the one good thing about getting old is that I played with the people I did.

· *10 January 1985* ·

Twenty years ago today I got married for the first time to the angelic-looking Cristina de Caraman. She had just turned twenty-one and we eloped to Elizabeth, New Jersey, where a friend had arranged for a judge to marry us. When we arrived in court, he was sentencing various petty criminals, but he took time out to give us 'life'. Which turned out instead to be three years long. I'm wondering what odds I would have given back then if someone had wagered me that twenty years to the day I would be in the same position that those people we had interrupted were in on 10 January 1965. A million to one? A billion?

I think about Cristina and her carefree life in Palm Beach where she now lives and instantly I start to feel sorry for myself. The trick in prison is never to think. As in tennis. The more you think, the worse you make matters for yourself. As Pavlo, my Cypriot drug-dealer friend, says, 'If you never think of the outside, you don't feel you're on the inside.' The thing to do, then, when the mind starts to wander, is to concentrate on improving one's immediate lot. Which means finding ingenious ways to economize. For example, a needle can split a match in half, vertically; thus forty matches in a box become eighty, and with forty matches one can begin to trade. Plastic bottles can be cut and their narrow ends become salt and pepper shakers, rags from the shops turn into tobacco pouches and the stiff inside of the toilet paper makes a joint holder.

This morning I finish *Decline and Fall*, which I have been reading for the second time. I asked for it in order to compare my plight with that of Waugh's hero, but this time I didn't enjoy the book at all, probably because the comic aspect is missing when the reader is doing time. Evelyn Waugh gives me the impression of a sinner trying to be a saint, just as Graham Greene does of a saint reaching hard to be a sinner. Waugh would have gone mad in the jug, Greene to the contrary. I play a game with myself, trying to guess which writer would fit into prison life easier, but soon give up because it makes me think of all the things they would be missing.

· *14 January 1985* ·

One month in the nick.

Looking back, it hasn't been all that bad. On the contrary, in fact. What have I learned about my fellow inmates? First, that prisoners are exceedingly quick to take offence. Second, that their chief characteristic is their irresponsibility and their propensity for violence. Also, to expect their abrupt shows of personality, born of their longing to *be somebody*, which only leads them to try to assert their individuality by being aggressive to other cons. And, of course, I've also learned about the prisoners' bitterness towards society.

No rehabilitation happens in jail. Just containment. We live, unfortunately, in the era of the excuse. There is always somebody in authority ready to rush in and explain why a crime was perpetrated. For those in authority, and inmates as well, can never admit that a crime is ever committed because someone is bad, greedy or malicious. Criminals commit crimes because they are misguided, disturbed or unhappy. This is what you hear on the rare occasions when prisoners admit that a crime took place. Most of the time they do not. I would guess that more than eighty per cent of the inmates think they were framed by the police.

I can offer no magic solutions for this sorry state of affairs and how to improve it, not even after one month of first-hand experience, but what does seem clear to me is that we need to search for both the culprits and the motives. The combination of urban decay, squalor, boredom and grinding poverty makes for crime. Most of my friendships in this place are with people who wanted to be somebodies and were too weak to really try. In their fashion, they did exactly what I did with my tennis. They do not, however, ask themselves any questions. Every time I get into this kind of discussion with Warren, he screams that I'm no one to talk, that my silver spoon disqualifies me, and, although I admit that he might have a point, he nevertheless conveniently forgets that there are billions of people who have not turned to crime, people who have never even had a copper spoon at birth.

The common understanding of evil is 'someone committing bad acts'. But it's wrong. Evil is someone *choosing* to do wrong and most criminals are under the impression that they're not committing a crime when of course they are.

Alex is a tall, beautifully built con who pumps iron regularly in the gym. He looks like a cross between Richard
Harris and Terence Stamp and has the best voice in the
'ville', as Pentonville is referred to by the *au courant*. When
he sings his songs, mostly Gershwin and Irving Berlin,
everyone in the gym quietens down and listens. A professional thief who has done a lot of time, Alex has that
serene look about him that people often do who have
tuned out long ago, but he also has the reputation of
being violent and extremely dangerous.

This morning he asks me to spot for him while he's
doing bench-presses. (This means standing over him and
helping him if he gets into trouble.) I consider it an honour
and soon we are deep in conversation about prison life.
Alex thinks Pentonville is the worst jail in the whole kingdom. Another man is pumping with us, a Scot named
John, who is getting out this week. He's a nice man in his
early forties, but he looks sixty. He tells Alex and me that
this is definitely his last time in the nick. He's going
straight. 'I'm getting too old to take it,' he explains.

While Alex is spotting for John, he suddenly rams a bar
down on John's head and then, without a word, walks
away and starts to do sit-ups. John is bleeding and dazed.
I run to get help from Frank Heavy and Andy Gordon.
Nobody says a word. Soon we have John all bandaged up

and on his way to the hospital. Then, again without a word,
Alex is escorted down to the punishment cells. The punishment cells, in the bowels of the jail, are like every other
prison cell with one exception. There is nothing inside. No
bed, no chair, no table. Only a potty. A prisoner there is
allowed nothing. He remains in his underwear for the
duration. He gets the same meals as the rest brought to
him; just before bedtime he is allowed to bring his bed
inside the cell. In the morning he slops out and puts the
bed on the landing. He gets nothing to read, no mail, no
contact with anyone. Prisoners may be kept in the punishment block for a maximum of two weeks. Which is what
the scuttlebutt says Alex will get.

On my way back to my cell for dinner, I find a book I
loaned Alex on my bed. He must have told the screw taking
him down that he had to return it, so the screw opened up
my cell and left it. How strange. Alex has just tried to kill a
man without any provocation and then he takes the time to
ask the screw to return a book to a man who Alex probably
believes will have to give evidence against him. Which is
one thing I plan not to do. It will not help poor John – who,
Frank Heavy tells me, is not badly hurt – and it will only
get Alex into more hot water than he's already in. So goes
a primary unwritten rule of the nick. No matter what
happens, you don't give evidence against a fellow con. At
any rate, the question is of no practical significance; Alex
will be moved to a long-term prison the moment he emerges
from below. I thank my lucky stars that I kept quiet and
said nothing about getting out or going straight while Alex
was spotting for me. He might well have dropped the
weight on my head instead of on poor John's. Did the 'ville'
finally get to Alex, is that why he did it? Or was it simply
Alex being Alex, as I, being Taki, had to call attention to
the contents of that fateful envelope at Heathrow Airport?

· *16 January 1985* ·

My old American friend from C-wing remarks that I've lost a lot of weight. No sooner does he say it than a screw arrives in the gym and takes him away to the punishment block. Frank Heavy later tells me that the Yank, as everyone calls him, had his cell searched and about fifty razorblades were found. It was searched because he was trying to organize the inmates to protest against Pentonville's unsanitary conditions. Poor Yank. He was immediately given away to the screws, more, probably, because he is a foreigner than because he tried to organize. (Once in the block, he broke down and begged for mercy and it was granted. By that afternoon, word spread that he was now working for the 'fuzz'. In view of his quick release, he undoubtedly was.)

I liked Yank when I was in C-wing, but eventually he got on my nerves by constantly quoting the *Guardian* to me and railing against the 'system'. Like everyone else he claimed to be innocent, which didn't bother me a bit, but what bothered me a lot was how he had politicized his incarceration, claiming to be a victim of capitalism. Moreover, he was in for fraud, which only meant he had indulged in an unacceptable aspect of capitalism, so, if anyone were to blame, it was himself. Once, when we were talking, I reminded him that in a socialist paradise he would undoubtedly have received five to ten years for defrauding the people, but he kept banging on about the fascist state. Oh well, he is now in cahoots with it, which should make his life considerably easier.

Before dinner I look at myself in the tiny wooden mirror I was issued with upon arrival and I'm appalled at what I see. I am drawn, deep circles are grooved under my eyes, my skin is green and scaly. It is the lack of sunshine, the bad food, the over-exercise. All compounded by the insufficient sleep. In addition, my whole body aches. I'm starting the flu.

• *17 January 1985* •

I feel terrible. All night I alternate between shivers and sweats. The cell is very, very cold, but my body is burning up with fever. At slop-out, I ask the kind Welsh guard, Mr Jones, whether I can stay in my cell and be excused from work, but it's no go. He sympathizes, but rules are rules. I can either go to the hospital or continue to work. To go to the hospital or to see the doctor I have to line up after breakfast for an application form, list my problem and wait for an answer. If one is lucky, the procedure takes at least two or three days.

Of course there is no way to go to the hospital with its Aids cases, where one is likely to catch a disease. By 'hospital', I mean a dormitory filled with fifteen beds instead of the required six, with one lavatory at the end. The beds are barely a foot apart and the smell of the place makes our landing by comparison seem to have been showered with all the perfumes of Arabia. I know this from Lee Anderson who spent a night there and Lee wasn't exactly brought up with all the comforts of the Waldorf.

Having the flu is always nasty, but in prison it's torture. You get no liquids, no warmth, no aspirin to relieve the pain, not even a little TV to alleviate the burning sensation in your head. (Fighting fire with fire.) The only liquid allowed in prison is tea, except for the water you can drink from the tap during slop-out which everyone else is using

to wash out their slop buckets. The last time I felt so
helpless was when I fell ill in Vietnam, so I try to think
back and remember that miserable experience, hoping
against hope that memory will make me feel better.

It was the second time I'd gone to that unhappy place.
The first had turned out to be a dud, with me walking
around Saigon interviewing American military spokesmen
who to a man told me what I wanted to hear. This time I
was determined to get a bit closer to the action and see for
myself. In the spring of 1972, forty NVA divisions had
broken through the DMZ, captured Quang Tri and were
poised to attack Hue, the old imperial capital lying on the
banks of the Perfumed River. I was writing for William F.
Buckley's *National Review* at the time, and Bill had
managed to get me accredited in no time. Once in Saigon I
quickly hitched a ride with the daily military plane shuttle
to Da Nang; from there it was a short helicopter flight to
Phu Bai, the American airbase. From Phu Bai I was on
my own, so I joined up with a *Stars and Stripes* correspondent with a jeep and we drove up to Hue.

Joe Fried had advised me to stay at The Hotel, as the
best hotel in Hue was called – in fact, he had told me in no
uncertain terms that The Hotel rivalled the Paris Ritz in
comfort and luxury. Knowing Joe's reputation as a prank-
ster I didn't bother to pack a dinner jacket, but I hadn't
realized how much of a joker he really was. The Hotel
turned out to be the place where the press spent the night.
This bombed-out building once upon a time, I am sure,
must have been a hotel, but in the spring of 1972 its only
resemblance to one was a roof, and a leaky one at that.
Needless to say, there was no service, no linen for the few
beds available, no food, not much more than the walls and
some gutted rooms, one of which I was lucky enough to

get. Most of the journalists were camping out in the lobby, or what was left of it. Hue had gone through a bloody battle in '68, had fallen to the Viet Cong–NVA who had slaughtered a large part of its population and then, after more street fighting, had been retaken by the Americans. By the time I arrived, most of the people had fled. Only the hookers remained, working out of small saipans down by the river.

No sooner had I bunked down for the night than malaria struck, or at least something closely resembling it. For three days I ran a high fever, and even became delirious for a while, but the *Stars and Stripes* buddy proved a saviour, filling me up with pills and aspirin. On the fourth day the fever disappeared as suddenly as it had struck, but the three days I lay sick in the 'Hue Hilton' I shall not soon forget.

For the next month I roamed the environs of Hue, helicoptering back and forth from Phu Bai to Da Nang and driving almost daily to Firebase Birbingham. I had been issued a helmet and bulletproof jacket, and while driving around in the jeep I got into the habit of wearing it around my crotch rather than putting my arms through it. My friend thought I was crazy, but there you are. It's each to his own when it comes to fears and I was absolutely paranoid about having my you-know-what blown up – or *off* – by a mine.

The commander of Firebase Birbingham was Colonel Mao, the most decorated soldier – perhaps I should say combat soldier – in the South Vietnamese army, or ARVN. He and I got along well and often talked well into the night about politics and the war. This simple man-boy from the Central Highlands, who already had a wife and children, was convinced that Uncle Sam would never leave him to his fate. I have often thought of him since, wondering whether he's alive or whether he died in some prison camp. Mao was very gung-ho and I know what Communists do with his kind.

Once it became obvious that the B-52s had given Charlie a very bloody nose and that Hue would not be attacked, I flew back to Saigon, where I reflected with nostalgia on the month I had spent in Hue and Firebase Birbingham. Although I had been in the middle of the action, I had seen almost no suffering. Hue was a ghost town and Birbingham a fortified camp. One saw the 105 howitzers blasting away all day and heard the rumble of the B-52s, but almost never came upon the mangled bodies. And, more important, the civilians weren't around. It was the kind of war we see – saw, rather – in the old movies. All glory, no pain.

Saigon was all pain.

I moved into the Palace Hotel where almost no journalists stayed. I don't like to run with the pack, especially a pack that by then was openly hostile to the war and spoke disparagingly about the South Vietnamese army and the American commanders. Most intolerable were some of the British hacks, William Shawcross especially, and whenever I met them in the army PX – where they all invariably hung out in pursuit of consumer goods furnished by Uncle Sam – I would be rude. So the Palace, further down from To Do Street, it was.

One day I noticed a pretty young girl hanging about in the lobby. I was having a drink with Gavin Young, the British writer and journalist, who is as attractive and knowing as he is a good writer. I said something about the girl's innocence (probably what I love most in a woman) and Gavin replied, 'Well, why don't you do her a favour and take her upstairs?' Yes, she was a prostitute and I did immediately ask her. After she produced her card for the concierge, he allowed her to come to my room.

I hate discussing or writing about sex almost as much as I like doing it, so I will spare you the details. Suffice it to say that when I moved towards her ever so gently, she repulsed me, raising her hands in a defensive gesture. I did not persist. In fact, I remember sitting down at my small desk, unzipping my portable typewriter and typing away. She sat by the bed briefly and then she got up and walked about the small room. From the corner of my eye I saw her open up my closet and look inside. Then she began to laugh and came over and hugged me. The inevitable happened, and later we went down for a drink. She spoke no French, a few words of English, and the only Vietnamese I knew was '*Bao-Chi*' – newspaperman.

After that, I saw her regularly. She came from Vung Tao, a so-called resort near the Delta, and she had a large family. One day she asked me in sign language to accompany her on a visit to them, still in Vung Tao. I agreed and we got into a Saigon taxi, a yellow-and-blue mini-Renault which may or may not have been pre-war vintage, and off we went. One hour out of Saigon I noticed the driver becoming increasingly jumpy. I asked him in French what was wrong and he answered, '*Beaucoup VC, beaucoup VC!*' So I yelled for him to turn back, and he did, executing the best U-turn I have ever had the privilege to witness.

But the little one protested and soon I could see big tears welling up in her eyes and then rolling down her cheeks. However many times I repeated that a little family visit wasn't worth getting shot for, she had one pat answer. 'Vung Tao, Vung Tao.' Eventually it dawned on me why she had gone through my closet and why she was so anxious to show me to her family. They probably didn't know she was a prostitute, and once she realized I wasn't a soldier – she had been roughed up by one – she was eager to show me off. So much for what war does to people. It makes them so desperate for things we take for granted that they willingly risk their lives just to show they stick out a bit from the rest. (Now, isn't that what I said just a little while ago about the nature of my prisonmates in Pentonville? Am I talking generally about what desperation and a certain degree of hopelessness do to people?)

But at that time I did not share those qualities with her. We never made it to Vung Tao, and soon I left Saigon.

Too much has been written about the war in Vietnam for me to add anything original, except to say that I shall never forgive nor forget what Jane Fonda and some of her cohorts did when they flew to Hanoi and called the American pilots held nearby 'war criminals'. The act was unspeakable, worse than treason, a tawdry publicity stunt, and an inhuman one at that. Those 'war criminals' were among the best men America has produced, the bravest of the brave, extraordinary men. They deserved better than the cages they got to call home for years on end, and far, far better than to be insulted by an actress who, after tiring of St Tropez and the fast lane, went on to embrace various self-promoting causes.

Yet times do come when one has to follow one's conscience before the rule of law. I do not dispute that. Still, civil disobedience does have its limits. Being photographed in a steel helmet in Hanoi is one of them. That's Hollywood's version of a conscientious objector, no different from a public relations exercise.

P S – And Ms Fonda's silence since the fall of Saigon over the re-education camps has, as they say, been deafening. Fonda, in a Cigarette speedboat off the coast of Vietnam, would not be a bad photo-opportunity to publicize the plight of the boat people, would it now?

The figures speak for themselves. Two million Indo-Chinese have braved death in order to escape persecution and famine.

· *18 January 1985* ·

I cough and shiver throughout the night. Whether it's a malaria attack or something akin to it doesn't matter, the symptoms are one and the same. I've suffered this every two or three years recently, and I make a solemn promise to myself that when I get out I will have myself checked out by the greatest expert in the world.

No news from the doctor's office, so I drag myself to the gym and go through the motions. Mr Heavy slips me some aspirins, but by now I'm sweating profusely, so he takes me to the infirmary and asks an Indian male nurse to have a look. He does so by asking me to describe my symptoms. Then he hands me some brownish liquid in a paper cup to drink in front of him. It turns out to be cough syrup. Mr Leggett, as senior officer, tells me to go back to my cell and stay there. It's against the rules, but I'm not about to argue.

While lying in bed I think of dissidents in totalitarian countries who go through prison and torture, deliberately. What kind of people must they be to put themselves in such a position intentionally? What possesses them? If they can do it, why can't I? Why am I at the end of my tether?

I guess it all has to do with accepting suffering for one's cause rather than suffering punishment for one's crime. Maybe I should try to convince myself that I was framed for my beliefs. Then my suffering would be over.

· *21 January 1985* ·

My application to see the doctor has been approved, but this morning I wake up feeling fine. No fever, no aches, just a lot of congestion in the chest. Amazing how well one feels once the fever has gone. It's all relative, as they say . . . If I hadn't had the fever yesterday, I'd be feeling pretty lousy this morning. As it is, I'm full of beans and raring to go.

After breakfast, while waiting to be unlocked and go to work, I look back at my forty-odd days in the nick and ruminate about how different prison seems now. During the first days Pentonville was an ugly, dirty and unfriendly place, full of baddies who demanded my constant vigilance. Now, despite some objectionable characters and a cruel guard or two, I feel at home here. Especially when I'm alone in my cell or in the gym. Mr Heavy and Mr Leggett, Mr Wrigley and Mr Holliday are like my uncles, and Lee, Warren and Trevor not unlike my brothers.

It feels good to train once again. Later, while taking the gym laundry down, Mr Leggett escorts me over to a corner window, where he tells me to step on a chair and look out. And, for the first time since entering prison, I see what the outside world looks like. Mr Leggett snickers while I stare at a parked red car for about a minute. 'See what you've been missing?' he asks. Judging from the street, a grubby and sad part of London, not much, but what the hell?

Having a prison directly in front of Harrods wouldn't be right now, would it? Why disturb all those nice folks who shop there?

After dinner, mail arrives, and lots of it. At least thirty letters and telegrams. The two funniest are a postcard from producer Michael White from, of all places, Bolivia – 'You wouldn't need to import anything *here*,' he writes – and from Gianni Agnelli, warning me to keep Vaseline handy. Gianni is a friend of long standing. In fact, I seem to have spent the better part of my youth on board one of his many boats or houses. He was an idol of mine when I was younger, probably still is, but I no longer follow him around like a dog. Which some people say I used to do. Although I'm not prone to such displays of adoration, I well recall how impressed I was by the ease with which Gianni handled his life, his imperturbability with his various mistresses, his agility at keeping his wife and family separate from his playboy persona, and I especially remember his wicked humour. Mind you, most people given Gianni's power and money would also find their lives less complicated. Or would they? One of the reasons Gianni insisted on having me around all those years was that he saw me as an innocent, an uncomplicated fellow. One of the few who wanted nothing from him but his company. Just before I came into this place, I visited him in the Connaught Hotel, where he was staying. Our meeting was strained. I was too embarrassed to relax and so was he. His wife hardly looked at me. I had committed the ultimate sin. I had been caught.

A letter from Tina Brown, the editor of *Vanity Fair*, for which I was writing a column that was discontinued as soon as I was arrested. She is sorry about the column, Tina writes, but, as it happened, she was out of town when the higher-ups got rid of it, and me. I presume she means Alexander Liberman, the overall fuehrer of Condé Nast publishing. But, Tina continues, she wants me back once I've paid my debt to society. I have my doubts, however. I am not sure my kind of writing will fit in with her plans. She is one ambitious lady. Still, it's the right sort of message to send someone in the jug.

I first met Tina when she took over as editor of *Tatler*. She popped into my house one morning and asked me to write a travel column for her. I agreed. Her rise was already meteoric. She had come down from Oxford and in almost no time landed the job of editor, following some extremely well-written profiles of famous and powerful establishment figures. It has been an upward curve ever since. I like Tina, but suspect there's a bit of Iago in her. Perhaps Iago is the wrong character. Uriah Heep, maybe. Actually, neither of these. Beneath Tina Brown's friendly exterior lies the slippery soul of Cardinal Richelieu.

In New York, arrogance goes with the territory. Perhaps it's sour grapes, but it's impossible for someone like me to understand people like Tina. They have talent, and yet they prefer stroking the rich and famous to challenging them. Tina once killed a story of mine about Mustique and Princess Margaret: two weeks later I read somewhere that she went visiting to Mustique and dined with the Princess. Ms Brown, married to a fine man and a good journalist, Harold Evans, has turned *Vanity Fair* into a celebrity mag, and a pretentious one at that. But, as many do with *People* magazine, I buy it, hide it between the covers of more literary publications and read it cover to cover.

My objection to celebrity magazines is that their journalism is not adversarial. They sometimes kick midgets, but never Goliaths. Personally, I can only write in a negative style where the rich and famous are concerned. As Renata Adler once said, 'I don't write against sensitive souls writing sonnets in a garret.' This is very important. No, more than important, it's one of the pleasures of my life, taking on those whom others arse-lick. Those whom *Women's Wear Daily* and Suzy of the *New York Post* treat as stars. As a friend of mine recently wrote in his letter to me, 'There must have been some glasses discreetly raised in New York the night you went in.' My only doubt concerns the discretion of their raising. I certainly don't blame them. After all, if it weren't for those who own bookshelves full of leather-bound, unopened classics, I would be out of business.

The irony is that in England I have no trouble whatsoever writing against those who would rather shop than eat. Over here, new money tries to emulate the old, thus avoiding the cheap tastelessness its American counterparts are famous for. *Nouveaux riches* Europeans, taking their cue from the way the aristocracy conducts itself, try to be friendly, relaxed and to talk about subjects other than acquisitions and money. *Nouveaux riches* New Yorkers and Californians, however, get their guidance from *Women's Wear Daily* and their decorators. In Europe one is judged more by the kind of person one is than by how respectably one behaves. So, despite the Old World's class system, I find that its people tend to feel less left out, probably because celebrity magazines and the gossip columns do not constantly remind them of how great the high and mighty are. On the contrary. Every aristocrat, business tycoon, powerful politician and celebrity is fair game, as they should be. People who seek the limelight cannot have it both ways. Although in America they sometimes do. What I would love to see is the manner in which some of the British social columnists would handle such

classic cases as Jerry Zipkin, the Gutfreunds and Alecko
Papamarkou, whose reputation and glamour (*glamour*?)
are based solely on the publicity their press agents put out.

Unfortunately, this will not happen in the great democracy that is America. The American people are too nice,
not at all envious and do not like to see their idols mocked.
(An Englishman will see a man driving an expensive car
and say to himself, 'One day we'll take that away from
him.' An American in a similar situation will say to himself, 'One day I'm going to have one, too.' Therein lies the
difference between the two cultures.)

I agree that idols should not be mocked as a matter of
course, but it depends on who the idols are. What the
social columns and celebrity magazines have created are
false idols. They are far too many for me to list, but a
random look at a Suzy column will give you some idea.
Take Zipkin, for example. I've known him for far too
long. Some of his friends swear by him, others are of a
different mind. He and I were civil to each other for years,
until I wrote an article predicting the kind of person Nancy
Reagan would invite to the White House. Although I'm
extremely conservative in my politics, I have never gone
along with Nancy the First's idea of an entourage for the
President of the United States. Dressmakers, jewellers and
interior decorators may be chic for the people *Vanity Fair*
profiles, but they are hardly the sort to inspire the leader
of the Free World. I predicted back in 1980 that Nancy
Reagan would surround herself with those incapable of
coherent expression or deep thought, except where gossip,
dressing and entertaining were concerned. Zipkin stopped
speaking to me.

And matters got worse when one night my great and
very old friend Reinaldo Herrera, a gentleman of the old
school if ever there was one, and his wife, the beautiful

and gentle Carolina, invited Alexandra and me, as well as Zipkin, to a dinner for Princess Margaret. At Mortimer's. I find PM, as her courtiers call her, an unappealing woman. She pulls rank, can seem rude and fulfils no visible function that I can see except to create envy and more class hatred. Worst of all, she's spoiled, constantly forgetting that she's nothing but a civil servant, or, at best, the sister of the highest-ranked civil servant of the United Kingdom. But that night I was most polite, as I had, after all, accepted the Herrera invitation. Carolina and Reinaldo had everyone take turns speaking to the Princess, and by the time my turn came to sit next to her I was quite wrecked. I tried to make conversation by reminding her that we had met in '67 – it came out 'shixty-sheven' – to which she, also well-oiled, snapped, 'What, you're a shivil shervant?'

'Do I look like a shivil shervant?' I answered.

Her response was, 'My God, he *ish* a shivil shervant.'

End of dialogue.

I quickly went back to my seat, but soon PM decided to leave and rose from her chair. That is when Mortimer's black piano player, obviously not versed in royal protocol, played a few bars on his organ of 'God Save the Queen'. 'No, no, let's have none of that,' hissed the Princess.

The chance was too good to miss, and despite my hosts' clear discomfort, I yelled, 'It's not meant for you, Ma'am. It's for Jerry Zipkin.'

One day, I imagine, when we look back upon the Reagan accomplishments, such as the re-arming of America and the cutting of punitive taxation, they will overshadow the shenanigans of his wife's friends. But the liberal press, which thrives on denying the good Reagan has done for the country, will always use the excesses of greedy social climbers as an 'only under Reagan' phenomenon. And of course it will be wrong. The social climbers, the greedy real-estate developers, the Wall Street sharks, were there long before RR. They had learned to buy expensive art in public, had tried to join prestigious cultural boards and had raised funds for the right charities while the peanut farmer was still being chased by giant killer rabbits. They were also cultivating the right editors and gossip columnists long before Nancy came to Mortimer's. In fact, I remember a dinner at Le Cirque, where my wife was seated next to John Gutfreund, the 'Clyde' to his wife's 'Bonnie' of social climbing, when the chairman of Salomon Brothers, as Gutfreund I believe still is, looked at my wife's earrings and told her how much he admired them. 'Thank you very much,' said Alexandra.

'I like them and I want to buy them,' said Gutfreund.

'I'm sorry, they're not for sale,' answered the wife.

That's when John Gutfreund, chairman of Salomon Brothers, summed it all up. 'Everything is for sale.'

I guess he was judging by his friends and his family.

Mail from Reinaldo Herrera, who for obvious reasons addresses me as 'My dear Monte Cristo.' His family settled in South America over four hundred years ago; his house, built in 1590, is the oldest continuously inhabited house in the Western hemisphere. His is a fine family, never known to speak ill of people or to put on airs. A real aristo Reinaldo is.

The next-to-last envelope I open reveals a large card from – my turn to name-drop – my close, very old friend, the Duke of Beaufort. It is a painting of his ancestral country seat, Badminton House, and all his family have signed it. Today, his only daughter, Anne, a historian of merit, is having a ball to celebrate her thirtieth birthday. She has written me a short note at the bottom, saying that she expects me never to speak to her again in view of her advanced age and my predilection for younger girls.

The last envelope holds a still larger card, signed by all the staff at Annabel's.

I go to sleep happy and content, and without fever.

Mail continues to pour in. Mr Jones tells me the governor has decided to make an exception and, in view of my being a writer and not a career criminal, will allow me to receive all my letters. 'The censors are furious,' says Mr Jones.

'Fuck the censors,' say I to no one in particular.

While pleased by the governor's magnanimity, I can't help thinking that even in jug there are prisoners and there are prisoners. Some of the letters, needless to say, are bound to raise eyebrows among the poor censors who have to read them, and for a pittance as salary. The Niarchos boys have written from their chalet in St Moritz and from the enormous floating gin palace anchored in Monte Carlo; the Guinnesses from their various grand houses in Tuscany and the English countryside; Lords Londonderry, Warwick and Hanson from the House of Lords (probably the most hated institution among guards and inmates alike) and Christopher Buckley (my best man) from the White House.

In all I've received about two hundred letters to date, but two of these will always stand out. The first came from a newspaper vendor in London, a Greek, C. Kotronis, who read about my plight while browsing through the *Spectator* and took the trouble to find out my whereabouts so he could write. He enclosed a religious picture in his epistle and offered some very good advice. Then he ended his letter, 'You're a Greek, and Greeks are not criminals by nature, but they do make mistakes. God bless you.'

The other is hand-delivered now, and by the chaplain himself. It has not been opened and the chaplain asks me to read it in front of him. It's from Richard Nixon. Once the chaplain is assured it's not a trick, he starts to leave and as he does I ask him why this letter was not censored. 'They are intimidated by it,' he answers, 'so they put it in the hands of a man of God.' He is smiling as he speaks, so I never do find out precisely why the special treatment. Are American ex-presidents like Caesar's wife?

President Nixon's letter is both encouraging and compassionate. Right then and there I decide to frame it and hang it on the most visible wall of my house. And speaking of compassion, there is a side of Richard Nixon which has never been written about, his tender side, although I don't expect those who hounded him from office to take my word for it. What I find most amazing about the Fourth Estate is its blindness when up against somebody or something they can – to use a Nixonian turn of phrase – 'kick around' with sanctimonious impunity. In my opinion, Nixon was guilty of one of the few crimes today's politicians cannot afford to commit, lack of charisma and charm. And, of course, getting caught. Yet, even before Watergate, he was deeply hated by those who make up public opinion in the great democracy that is America, by the very same people who knew what the Kennedys were up to while in the White House, and who turned a blind eye and a deaf ear to it. It's that double standard again, inexplicable. The press, for example, always held Nixon responsible for the vicious red-baiting of Helen Douglas, yet it has just as viciously 'blue-baited' him long after his fall from power. And the fact that he will never sue – and that as a public figure he cannot – has not slipped their minds. Nixon is fair game to anyone who doesn't agree with him. I imagine his going after Alger Hiss did not win him any friends, either.

Hiss was the US state department official who denied passing 200 secret documents to the Communists before a Congressional Un-American Activities Committee, on which Nixon sat. He was tried twice for perjury and convicted in 1950, despite various high-ups, including Adlai Stevenson, testifying to his good character. I had a strange encounter with him not long ago. The *Spectator* holds bi-weekly lunches and for one of them Eric Jacobs, a *Sunday Times* journalist, brought Hiss. I was seated next to him and told him during the course of our conversation that I had a political trial coming up in Greece and was hoping that Bill Buckley would write something in my defence, as the Greek courts were aware of foreign public opinion. I then turned and began to converse with Charlie Douglas-Home, the editor of *The Times*. That is when I heard Hiss telling his neighbour what a terrible man Buckley was, not to help this nice young fellow from Greece. I had said nothing of the sort, but there was this old gentleman lying right in front of me, without even bothering to keep his voice down. At once I realized that Hiss is not confined by the rigours of fact, that unwittingly he relaxes them, confusing his wishes for reality.

Which brings me back to Nixon.

I believe it has been proven beyond doubt that Hiss was guilty as hell, but the Nixon-haters will have none of it. Although we are at the very point in history when the common man has assumed a social primacy of sorts, the leftists find the common man too vulgar, too nationalistic, too patriotic, too suspicious of crusading spirits, to be taken seriously. They dismiss him as a redneck, a fascist, a know-nothing. If you substitute Nixon for the common man, you have my apologia for the thirty-seventh President of the United States. (And see, in part, why he's hated by the media.)

And even if this is all wrong, even if Nixon were the scourge the liberals said he was, why pursue Javert-like a man who was already driven from power? A man who has conducted himself quite well, ever since? His flawed character, his scarred conscience, have been held aloft in public throughout the globe now for years. Yet how many acknowledge that few could have achieved what he did, be flexible as well as strong with the Soviet bloc and offer the substantial degree of seriousness he did regarding foreign policy? That Nixon erred is no secret. That his errors were disastrous, going against, as they did, the fundamental concepts of democracy in America, is no secret either. His imperfections are well known. His assets, however, are just as well kept hidden, especially by the press. I don't recall reading anything about his resilience, his strong mind and complex personality. Yet those qualities exist.

In short, the very compassion Nixon's critics claim he lacks has been notably absent on the part of those who continue to malign the man.

Moreover, the crime Nixon was accused of was the cover-up of the break-in; he flouted the rule of law. On this point the media shows its noxious double standards nowhere clearer, nowhere smelling more foul, than in the treatment of Teddy Kennedy's cover-up at Chappaquiddick and his subsequent drunken behaviour.

I met Nixon through Bob Tyrrell, the editor of the *American Spectator*, a good friend of long standing. I still remember word-for-word something Nixon said to me at that first meeting. 'One can be a patriot without being a warmonger and one can be for peace without being a traitor.'

It made sense then and it makes sense now.

What make no sense at all are a couple of other statements of Nixon's, direct quotes I read somewhere and also committed to memory. The first: 'In all my years of public life I have never obstructed justice.' Can *any* powerful political figure say that and mean it? Would any *sensible* powerful political figure even dare try?

The second: 'When the President does it, that means it is not illegal.'

Well, say no more.

But I must confess I know the feeling. It is not uncommon among us privileged folk, but it is delusional. I look up at the bars of my cell. They testify to that.

Yet Greeks are well acquainted with hubris and its temptations. Quakers are not supposed to be.

• *26 January 1985* •

On my way to the gym this morning I dropped a piece of paper near the garbage can rather than in it, and a screw called Scanlon yelled at me to 'Retrieve that at once!' Scanlon has treated me generally in a vile manner. He is one screw who likes being a screw and throwing his weight around, so I try to pull his leg a bit and ask him where in the world did he learn such a long word as 'retrieve'?

Well, Frank Heavy did warn me about being sarcastic with the guards as well as the cons. Both groups hate nothing more. Frank thinks it has something to do with their general insecurity and the fact that they know they aren't exactly practising a profession that is sought after by intelligent men.

I should have listened to him. No sooner did I open my big mouth than Scanlon – a huge man – is on me, grabbing me by the back of my neck and forcing my head down to the floor. He is shouting insults and threatening me with the block. Although I feel deeply mortified, I say nothing and do even less. Guards are known to fake taking a shot in the gut and then retaliate by sending the prisoner to the block for the maximum two weeks. It is what Scanlon is hoping for, but I ain't about to oblige.

Once he lets go of me, I throw the paper inside the can and begin to walk away, but he comes at me again and orders me to stand at attention facing the wall. In the meantime, all the cons are on their way to work and stare at the spectacle. I swallow hard, but follow Scanlon's orders to the letter. While waiting at attention, I think how in the past I reserved my ridicule for the more 'progressive solutions' to the problem of criminal reform. Now the shoe is on the other foot and I don't like it a bit. In fact, I am standing here and contemplating the injustice of imprisoning people for any crime short of multiple murder.

After about an hour, Frank Heavy comes and gets me and I go to the gym. Warren, Trevor and Lee are there and in no uncertain terms they accuse me of being a coward, of playing footsie with the enemy. I get furious and tell them to go and fuck themselves, but I feel ashamed and terribly humiliated.

How literature and the movies have romanticized criminals! We are expected under pressure to act like honourable men, yet the very fact that we have committed a crime – a dishonourable condition – is almost always overlooked. I like those three, Warren, Trevor and Lee, but I think they're being intolerant. What was I supposed to do? Fight with Scanlon, get thrown in the block and lose my remission? To prove what? And yet, and yet . . . They have a point; though philosophically I am right. Jailers traditionally reduce prisoners to an 'it'. Politically, this inequity is what makes a fascist state. For fascist states maintain themselves by the denuding of personality. The needs, the rights, the interests of the individual are forever subordinate to those of the state. And psychologically it is even worse. In one short hour Scanlon robbed me of my manhood, reduced me from a name to a number, reduced me to a child. Whether childhood is rich or poor, good or bad, emotionally healthy or otherwise, children suffer the tyranny of adults. In jail, prisoners are children and guards adults. And, as in childhood, all power lies with one side. Some people crave that. They want to be cared for at any price. They remain helpless and dependent. For them jail is freedom.

But it is not a wish most of us share. Least of all myself. Yet my three friends just made me feel as if I were one of 'those', and I feel frustrated, impotent, filled with hatred. I swear I'll get Scanlon one day.

Then, calming down, I think of those political 'dissidents' of our free society, and how their perversion of the word 'fascist' insults those who have suffered, and are still suffering, in closed societies, and my anger turns from Scanlon to those who call America 'Amerika'. A fascist state. Scanlon, after all, is like most cops anywhere. But only the Third World sanctions their brutality, putting it squarely in the service of their governments. As policy.

· *29 January 1985* ·

The letter I've been dreading has arrived. It's from my old man. I leave it for last and then start to read the newspapers, but it doesn't work. I'm too nervous to read, so I open it and immediately know that everything will be all right.

My father first heard of my bust through the Greek newspapers. When he rang me in London I told him the stuff had been planted on me. I was too ashamed to tell him otherwise. Not afraid, mind you, but ashamed. He believed me without reservation. Ironically, someone had planted dope on him during the German occupation and then given him away to the Gestapo, but that had been an obvious plant and he was released almost immediately.

His letter is full of historical examples about perfidious Albion. Once I am out, he assures me, he will make certain the world hears about British justice. It is probably the nicest letter I've ever had from him.

My relationship with my father has been mostly based on fear. Until 1968, when he read in the newspapers that I had won the Greek all-comers karate championship, it was fear of physical violence. After that, and to my eternal shame I might add, there was the constant dread of being cut off financially. However ghastly it sounds, there is no other way to put it.

Not that I'm unique in that regard. On the contrary.
Greek fathers are not famous for spending their time
patiently explaining life's complexities to their children.
They operate, instead, from a vantage point of 'father-
hood', some combination of biological paternity, their experience of life and the knowledge they have garnered
from that experience. A child is told how things stand in
black-and-white terms. Ever since I can remember, in fact,
my father told me things, he never explained them. 'So-
and-so was a coward, a good-for-nothing', or else, 'a man
to respect'. He gave pronouncements, never the reasoning
behind them. His word was all I needed.

My father would have found it unthinkable to have
acted differently. His own father was the quintessential
tyrant, a rich landowner who sired many children out of
wedlock and forced my father to leave home while still in
his teens. My father's crime? Insubordination. An aunt
took him in, but later made him pay rent. Nevertheless,
he survived and prevailed, and in ten years he was a
millionaire industrialist.

His family came from Zante, an Ionian island which for
a time had belonged to Venice, and later, briefly, to England. His family were titled, but the old man scorned such
snobberies. When he set eyes on my mother and began to
pursue her, her family was appalled. He was reputed to be
the biggest womanizer in Greece. He finally got the family
to agree to him by putting a false announcement of be-
trothal in the newspapers. At that time, since the couple
already knew each other, publishing a denial would have
meant a scandal. Once married, he began to philander
almost immediately.

After my brother and I were born, my mother decided
never to go out again. I think she felt humiliated and
betrayed, but she has never complained or explained.

When the war broke out, my father left for the front; I still remember the revolting smell when he came home on leave and took off the boots he'd been wearing for months on end in the snows. After the front collapsed, he became a resistance leader. When the constant Anglo-American bombing would terrify me to tears, I still recall him looking disapprovingly at a six-year-old's fear. But I also vividly remember his coolness under fire, especially during the civil war.

When the Reds blew up his factories, he never once complained. It was the bleak winter of 1944, and Athens was one great cemetery. Still, he managed to get watches for my brother and me. In fairness to him, I must explain that in those days fathers confidently believed that, as long as they fed their children properly, protected them and gave them the proper advantages, they would grow up well.

After I was thrown out of Lawrenceville for being violent, I spent a harrowing three days waiting for him to come and get me. I had seen his temper before and was not looking forward to it. But when he heard the reason for my dismissal, he smiled at me and said, 'I thought you had done something unmanly.'

Throughout the next thirty years, my father hardly spoke to me, except to find fault with my lifestyle. He grew increasingly disenchanted with my tennis once it became obvious that my manners, not my strokes, might rival those of McEnroe today. Nevertheless, he continued to support me in the style to which I was accustomed.

When I began to write, he was equally discouraging. 'A dilettante's pursuit', he called it, and perhaps he was right. But he did confide to friends that he was proud of the reporting I did for a Greek daily from Vietnam and the Middle East.

He still treats me like a five-year-old and gets extremely embarrassed when I sometimes get drunk and tell him I love him. He has already informed my eight-year-old daughter that she and her brother will inherit half his fortune, and that they should depend solely on him. He never ceases to remind me that my greatest accomplishment was fathering my two children.

I write this rather mortifying confession because I recognize how much he means to me, and did from the start. I realize, too, that, if he had spanked me more often instead of showing his irritation by lengthy disapprovals, I would not have minded. Spanking a child still means the child has possibility; lengthy disapprovals banish a child, ending possibility. But my father did both. That is why I cannot understand why I have always loved him and admired him, and can imagine life without my mother, a saint, but not without him. I suspect it's because he has given me the right priorities in life. Despite his shortcomings, his strength alone made him a good father. I hope it has made me one, as well.

They say that, to write a good work of fiction, one has to metaphorically kill one's father. Well, I guess I will never write the great American novel. And I don't care. My old man has been the one constantly dominating figure in my life, and it has nothing to do with money, either. He was, and still remains, the single person I've been forever trying to impress. He always will be.

When I finish reading my father's letter, I think of my brother Harry. I have not heard from him in years. I was told that members of his wife's family were furious that I had been arrested. If so, I'm almost glad I was. My brother and I are very different. He likes respectability and an ordered life, and is quick to take offence at anything I write. I once made fun of his lack of marksmanship, and he not only stopped speaking to me for years, but tried to get me fired from my job as columnist. He is plainly angry that I have tarnished the family image by getting thrown into the slammer, but what can I do about that? Instruct him in the proper care and treatment of a brother? Tell him that loving your brother means wanting *him* to be well and happy, not being concerned about how well and happy *you* would be, if only your brother would shape up?

Prisoners have enormous egos. Especially black prisoners. They're always telling you either about themselves or about how to do something the correct way, *their* way, of course. This morning, Atkinson, a large West Indian with an albino streak and known as one of the strongest men in the nick because of the incredible weight he can bench-press, is watching me do a reverse kick, my favourite karate technique. Although he knows little about the martial arts, he has to amble over and give advice. I listen politely, then keep doing it my way. He insists, until finally I am forced to tell him he doesn't know what he's talking about. So he switches to some sociological bullshit about how people like me, because of my background, are not willing to learn. Learn *what*? His brutality, or the mindless, scatological argot of jail life?

Atkinson is not necessarily unfriendly, but he's violent and has a quick temper. He's more aggressive than most, but then so are a lot of the blacks in Pentonville. I don't know the exact figures of the racial/ethnic background here, as no one is about to inform us on such matters, but it looks as if one third of the inmates is black – this in a country whose black population is three per cent.

Warren and I never stop arguing about the apathy and hostility of the black in a white society. Warren gripes that the state is racist by nature and does little for the black

man. His most vicious and colourful adjectives are reserved
for Mrs Thatcher and her 'rely on yourself' mentality. I
argue that, on the contrary, the blacks, especially in America, have been sandbagged by the welfare programmes
of Johnson's Great Society, programmes which have led to
the paralysis of the underclass, to their sloth, dependency
and self-contempt, as well as to poverty pimps.

Needless to say, I have not managed to convince
Warren, which doesn't in the least surprise me. What does
surprise me is his unwillingness to listen to something that
makes sense. After all, Warren is intelligent and shrewd.
Yet he refuses to see the absurd trap of the welfare system
– in America, especially – where free health care is available only to those on welfare, and taken away from them
the moment they land a job.

Warren's family broke up in the sixties and he grew up
with a variety of 'stepfathers'. It's obvious to me that his
problems have cultural, as well as economic, roots. The
effects of transitory values, such as free love and drugs,
did as much harm to the blacks as to the affluent white
society. Blacks had an unstable community to begin with.
I say all this to Warren, but he just continues his tedious
barrage of insults against the whites. It is like a Beckett
play. Or, better yet, something of Kafka's.

When it's time for a shower, I make sure to keep Atkinson in front of me. Warren and Trevor are egging him on,
but if he does get violent I know they'll restrain him. The
others pretend not to hear anything. Most try to cultivate
cynicism, probably for protection against prison's constant
rubs, so after a while I tell Warren, Trevor and Atkinson,
'You're just a bunch of motherfuckers.'

They laugh and the incident is over.

· *3 February 1985* ·

Mr Jones, a Welshman, and one of the nicest of screws, comes into my cell before dawn and tells me to get dressed. My immediate reaction is that I'm headed for the punishment block, but for what, I haven't the foggiest. Perhaps it's only a body-and-cell search, which means I might get the block for all the extra books, shirts and socks I've managed to collect by cheating at the laundry and the library.

As it turns out, it's nothing of the sort. A Greek prisoner has gone bonkers – he arrived last night – and they need an interpreter. The Greek, who is next to my old cell on D-1, is trembling and crying. He tells me he suffers from claustrophobia and that he will kill himself unless he's put in with another Greek. However awful it sounds, I don't pity him nor do I believe him. But I do translate verbatim, and Mr Jones and Wrigley tell me that he will be moved that afternoon, in with a Greek-speaking inmate. (Pavlo, as it happens.)

The Greek is in for pimping. He's got a long record, he tells me, and has done time in Greece where, he claims, conditions are far better. Greek prisoners can associate freely with others, relatives are allowed to bring in food and buggery is rampant. While telling me all this, he continues to snivel and cry, all for the benefit of the guards. Finally, I ask him to show some dignity. 'Please don't make us Greeks lose more face than we already have.' I wish him good luck and then I'm returned to my cell. Mr Jones asks me what I think, but I merely shrug and mumble something about nine million Greek actors.

In the gym, Frank Heavy tells me a funny story. Apparently the newsagent's shop across the street does brisk business every visiting day when relatives buy glossy magazines like *Vogue* and *Country Life*. Frank says that many of his charges are housebreakers and 'collectors' of art in the form of silver, trinkets and baubles, and furs. By reading the 'glossies', they keep abreast of salesroom trends and prices, as well as their plans for which mansion they will visit upon release. Which means that *Vogue* and other Condé Nast products do have a redeeming social value, after all. They are not published, as is sometimes suggested, purely for the pleasure of very rich old bags and to further fatten the Newhouse family's pockets.

After dinner, which is particularly vile today, Paddy, an old geezer, goes crazy and breaks up his cell. He smashes the bed, the chair, the table and his cellmate's jaw. It takes twenty screws to subdue him and carry him down to the block. He has five days to go before his release. The veterans blame Paddy's behaviour on 'gate fever', meaning the increased frustration of being nearly free. I'm not so sure. Paddy always looked a bit unstable to me, as I suppose anyone would who kept talking to objects such as my punching-bag, which Paddy often did.

· *4 February 1985* ·

A letter from Alexander Chancellor, the former editor of the *Spectator* and the man who first gave me my column eight years ago. He informs me that the world's greatest weekly has been bought by the Fairfax group of Australia, which as he points out is good news because they're very up-market types, as well as loaded.

Alexander is something of an enigma. He affects great vulnerability, yet he gets things done like no other. He is laid back almost to an unacceptable degree, but he never misses an appointment or a deadline. He thrives on playing the loser, but shows very few actual defeats on his professional and personal scorecard. He is also decent. He received a lot of flak when my column first appeared, but stood by me. After about a year, with my prose nearly on a par with that of TV personalities in America and the subject matter staler by the minute, he reluctantly decided to fire me. The trouble was, I wasn't around and Alexander did not wish to fire me through the mail. So he held the matter in abeyance while waiting for me sooner or later to drop by his office. Meantime, my prose improved somewhat and the column remained. I chanced to hear about my near-firing years later and asked Chancellor about it one night in Mortimer's while we were both dead drunk. Yes, came the answer, he would have done it in a minute, if only he had been able to find me.

When in 1983 Chancellor's turn came to be fired, most of the contributors resigned in protest, but then immediately demanded their letters of resignation back when they found out that Chancellor had signed on as the *Spectator*'s television critic. As always, even after being fired by Algy Cluff, our then proprietor, Chancellor got his way. He insisted that Charles Moore, the political editor, become top man and Charles got the job. Cluff wanted to appoint Germaine Greer to the post, but Alexander pointed out to him that the *Spectator* readership would not put up with a vagina on the cover.

Alexander finishes his letter in his usual ironic manner: 'The reasons, dear Taki, so many people want to buy the *Spectator* are that its writers are in prison, drunk, mad, or both, yet many feel it has tremendous influence on the great British public.'

The second letter, however, brings very bad news. It's from my wife, Alexandra, and it hits me like the proverbial ton of bricks. Her cold but polite note informs me that she has reluctantly decided to divorce me 'for the good of us both'. She ends by wishing me all the best and asking me to mend my ways once out of prison. My first reaction is to bang on the door and ask for a guard. In a little while I realize it's useless and sink into a deep depression. Unable to read or think, I pace up and down. All sorts of wild ideas race through my head, ideas filled with hatred, anger and revenge, as well as remorse. If only I could get out of this hellhole, I could make her change her mind. I think about it late into the night. Alas, there is no mystery as to why she has come to this decision. It's been a long time brewing.

I first heard of Her Serene Highness Princess Alexandra Schoenburg-Hartenstein while leafing through a French glossy some twenty-odd years ago. The article concerned the young scion of an old and noble family of Austria (the founder was Ulricus de Schunenberg in 1130) who was starting to work for French *Vogue* fully 830 years after her ancestor had made his mark in society. The accompanying photos showed me at once that the girl's looks did not belie the grand name and title. Aristocrats in Europe are inbred and tend to look it. They have pinched faces, no chins and resemble Pinocchio. Not, however, Her Serene Highness, here. She looked Latin, which her mother is, and beautiful and vital, with none of that flat, washed-out appearance that typifies so many of her dreary Austrian cousins. I made it a point to meet her and soon managed it. We did not hit it off right away. She was rather liberal, as young privileged girls tend to be, and, worse, she thought I was a male chauvinist, which I am, proudly. She also found it shocking that I, a man about to be married, quickly proclaimed my love for her and warned that she would one day marry me.

Well, as it happened, my prediction came true. Despite the objections of her mother, who was less than pleased to find her daughter running around with a divorced playboy. Nor did we have, Alexandra and I, exactly a conventional wedding. After my first marriage broke up, we began to see a lot of each other. By 1975 we had our first child, a girl, followed in 1980 by our second, a boy. In 1981 we married.

Our marriage was no more conventional; my fault, I admit. Did I inherit the Don Juan syndrome from my old man, a great philanderer, or did I develop it in self-defence? I don't know. What I do know is that I've always been obsessed with women, I've always been in love. Romantic love, they say, is by its nature delusional and brief, a fine madness. I agree. It also thrives on obstacles and danger, and this is the part that excites me. In reality, romantic love is like a sport, with the same built-in excuses for failure surfacing all over again. Or perhaps it is simply an age-old antidepressant. Nature's way.

Far-fetched? I think not. Love is ontological, *being* in its most vivid state, and nothing is more vivid than the start of a love affair. The faint whisper of hope, concealed inside the newly erotic. The promise of healing one's own dark injuries. A promise forever elusive.

I'm no philosopher. The mysteries of why people fall in love, stay in love, escape me. I only know that when I am not in love, I am as gloomy and ill-tempered and boring as the intellectuals who try to define love in every tedious aspect, physiologically, economically, psychologically, oh, you know . . . Words, words, words.

My father's favourite passage from Byron says, 'All tragedies are finish'd by a death,/ All comedies are ended by a marriage . . .' and so on. I prefer the same poet's simple truth about the difference between the sexes: 'Man's love is of man's life a thing apart,/ 'Tis woman's whole existence.'

No, in conventional terms, I have not been the best husband. Which has nothing whatever to do with the fact – ah, the age-old protest – that I do love my wife. That I do love our children. That we are joined. To that idea, I have always been and will always be faithful.

Back in 1981, I wrote a light and rather simplistic essay for the *American Spectator* called 'American Women Are Ugly Lovers'. The title was not mine but the editor's, R. Emmett Tyrrell, and the content had nothing to do with the sexual act but with those who preach and practise role reversal, no more, no less. Not surprisingly, my article caught the attention of feminists and all hell broke loose. As I happen to believe entirely in the equality of the sexes where jobs and salaries are concerned, I was unprepared for the reception I got when I appeared on the *Phil Donahue Show* in September 1982. Donahue I found to be an ignoramus without precedent. He was the most cliché-ridden, predictable man I've ever argued with, and argue we did. Phil is fiercely proud to be a 'feminist', but when I reminded him that people like me, so-called 'male chauvinists', rarely abandon a woman after she's borne him four children, he turned beet-red with anger. This liberated male, this Phil Donahue, had recently dumped a wife and four children to marry a starlet, an act I found, and still find, inconceivable. His marital fidelity – in his new marriage, in his former one – is to me immaterial. That he left his ageing wife is to me all-important. At least in the society where I grew up we honour and respect women, we protect them and provide for them, and, of course, we cuckold them at will. Different cultures, different values? There's not the smallest doubt in my mind about which is ethically superior.

Finally, I force myself to try to sleep. My family is about to break up, I tell myself once again, although I vow, before closing my eyes, not without a fight.

· 6 February 1985 ·

I am still having great trouble sleeping. It seems that one of the mysteries of the human body is the pineal gland, situated at the base of the brain. It secretes melanin into the bloodstream at night, which delivers the psychological signal for darkness. Thus the biological clock can tell the difference between the seasons and make other similar distinctions. Or something like that. At any rate, since I haven't been outdoors for more than two months, my biological clock has gone whacky. Sleep does not come easily. Getting bad news from home, plus the routine cruelty of prison life, doesn't help either. Moreover, I am beginning to suffer from 'gate fever', or so Warren tells me.

Pentonville is literally a cesspit. The wasteful idleness of prison life has everyone – staff and inmates alike – on edge at all times and, despite the popular conception that one can and does get used to everything, the stench of excreta is as unbearable to me today as it was at first whiff. This morning, William, a black in the next cell, usually a quick-witted *agent provocateur* and a wise guy, refuses to get out of bed. Two screws go in and start to drag him out. While they struggle with him, he yells to me to make sure I tell his story when I get out. I nod yes, but there is no story. It's just prison life getting to yet another inmate.

I finish Arthur Koestler's *Scum of the Earth*, a wonderful

book about incarceration and the writer's troubles with the French bureaucracy. What a rotten race the French can be! To think that they handed over thousands to the Gestapo, thousands of exiles, that is, when they didn't have to. And to think how I lived and spent so much money there for ten years, and loved every minute of it. But never again. Papa Hemingway compared Paris to a mistress who's always taking new lovers. He was right. Paris is a place to live in, to fall in love in, when one is young. Having done both there, I have no wish to return. The French are unpleasant – extremely well-read and intelligent, but complex, cruel and self-centred. They are also moral cowards. The moment I finish Koestler, I start on a biography of Marie-Antoinette, just to inflame further my already raging French sentiments.

· 8 February 1985 ·

Spiro, the monolingual latest Greek arrival, has been trying to find out my last name from Pavlo, his cellmate, but the Cypriot swears to me he hasn't told him. In fact, when Spiro asks me what my profession is, I say I'm a waiter in a north London restaurant, and that I'm in for stealing. The reason I have downgraded my station but upgraded my crime is that I fear Spiro's spilling the beans to the Greek press, once he returns to the birthplace of selective democracy. As I've said before, there is nothing more vicious or as mendacious as the Greek press and I already have visions of banner headlines proclaiming TAKI WAS THE MALE WHORE IN MY WING, subtitled SPIRO TELLS ALL!

Spiro is a pimp by profession and I wouldn't put anything past him. (The nicest name the Greek press has called me, to date, is 'traitor', for refusing to blame the CIA for our self-induced disasters, so I don't think the Greek hacks would hesitate to make up any story that suited their purpose.) Although Greeks are self-destructive, they are almost never dumb, and Spiro spends his time trying to figure out who and what I am. At least, so he tells me. He claims that waiters don't have my accent or the ability to resist saying *gamoto* (fuck) every other word.

As my bad luck would have it, it's Pavlo, not Spiro, who is the cause of trouble. About a week ago, during gym, one of the remands approached me, slipped me a small package for Pavlo, and walked away without saying another word. Although I'm supposed to be searched when I go in and out of the gym, it rarely happens because I'm the orderly. I took the grass (because that's what it was) back to Pavlo, who thanked me and, he later reported, spent a 'wonderful night' smoking away. So wonderful, in fact, that he must have bragged about it because this morning, after gym, a large Dutchman comes up to me and asks me to bring him some goodies, too. My immediate reaction is to deny that I ever brought anything out from the remands, but Munemann, as he's called, is one bad dude. He is also, I am told, a Mas Oyama karate devotee, doing twelve years for drug smuggling. He is in the 'ville' because he is being tried on another charge. Munemann is very big and tough and feared around the jail. I try to be as polite as possible without showing fear, but he tells me in no uncertain terms that, unless I get him some dope, he will slit my throat.

Pavlo denies he's said anything, but I know he's lying. I ask him for advice on what to do about Munemann, but Pavlo looks suddenly uninterested in my problem. I cannot go to the governor because Munemann hasn't actually done anything to report; furthermore, if I do, I'll be labelled a stool-pigeon and everyone in the nick will be after me. I decide to play for time and hope for something to happen to him. Or to me. Like someone slipping me a knife. But, unlike American prisons, there are absolutely no weapons inside Pentonville. I guess it will come down to fighting with one's hands and feet, and I am no match for Munemann in that department. Or so they tell me.

In all truthfulness, I loathe fighting. I used to do a lot of it because I was insecure and showing off, but, in recent years, I've generally walked away from fights. My last fight, however, was a lulu. It started at Mortimer's, the chic bistro on Lexington Avenue in New York City. I was part of a large and noisy dinner party, which included three close friends of mine, Andrew and Randall Crawley, and Olivier Chandon. (All three have since died tragically: Chandon, the champagne heir, while racing a car, the two Crawley brothers while flying their private plane.) Also among us were Virginia Warner, daughter of Senator John Warner of Virginia and Elizabeth Taylor fame, and Maura Moynihan, offspring of Daniel Patrick Moynihan of the State of New York. And CoCo Brown, a one-time Rhodes scholar and dabbler in real estate. CoCo is an awfully nice fellow, but rather controversial in business.

I only realized how controversial when suddenly, in the middle of dinner, an object came crashing down on our table, sending glass flying everywhere. As it happened, no one was hurt, but some of the girls present began to scream, so some of the men jumped up to look for the person who had thrown what turned out to be a heavy ashtray. We didn't have to look for long. A large man with a blond crew cut, dressed in black leather, stepped forward and insulted CoCo. By an ironic coincidence, he, too, was a Dutchman. His name was Jurgens. I did not know him, and, worse, I was unaware that he was an experienced karate practitioner and body-builder. After a lot of pushing and shoving, Jurgens called us a bunch of crooks and walked away without the slightest apology to the ladies present. It was time for my trick. Which is to go up to the person who is making warlike noises and politely ask him to step outside into a dark alley without anyone else being told. It's a good trick because most people would rather talk than fight. But this time it backfired. In fact, it had the opposite effect on Jurgens. With a thin, vicious smile, he thanked me in thickly accented English for the opportunity, ending with, 'Yes, I would luff to.'

Now there is only one key to winning a street fight. Hit first, and continue to hit until the opponent drops. Then kick him when he's down, and continue to kick until he stops moving. You begin by recognizing that sparring and tournament fighting are totally unrelated to self-defence and hand-to-hand combat. The former involves rules – and the safety you feel within those rules, however violent the sport – while the latter is about the survival of the fittest.

In the street, then, the faster you end a fight, the better. If there is no possible way to avoid trouble, you are well advised to explode at once, before your adversary gets a chance to realize what's hit him. You should *never* take a stance, *never* get set. You must not hesitate, hold back, delay or pause, even for a second. You attack, blast the adversary – on target – and keep on driving the attack until you render him helpless.

The Green Berets have a rule of thumb that says if you cannot win within thirty seconds, you will not win. Ninety-five per cent of preparing to win a street fight is mental. Most normal people would never dream of propelling themselves into a violent attack – simply because they are normal and do not want to fight. Too many decent people confuse this healthy reluctance to do battle with cowardice. It is nothing of the sort. If a person is eager to fight, anxious to inflict injury and joyful at the prospect of hurting others, he obviously isn't normal. Something is dangerously wrong.

The martial art student is trained to restrain himself psychologically. He programmes his mind beforehand; confronted by a violent attacker, he will press the offensive and win. In my case that night, better said than done. But with an excuse. After all, though he had agreed to step outside, Jurgens had not attacked. Once we were in the street, I bluffed further by asking him to go to 75th Street, where there was less light and far fewer people. Again he smiled that thin, malicious smile. And he charged with a front kick. I blocked it easily. But then, typically, I immediately reverted to type and baited him by saying he's got to do better than that. Alas, he did. He threw a round kick I never saw which crashed against my jaw, sending me down. Then it was his turn to make a mistake. Instead of stomping me, he bent down to grab me and I tied him up in a stranglehold. Fear can make people freeze, but it can also make them improvise brilliantly. I was soon choking him out and, as often happens when two equals fight, we quickly called it a night.

Needless to say, I came out of it looking much the worse for wear, while he didn't even have a hair out of place. By the time the rest of the party found us, my jaw had blown up to twice its normal size and my spirits were sagging. I shook hands with Jurgens and bade everyone else good night. The irony of it was that I found out the next day that CoCo had run off with the girl I'd had my eye on, which only proves that Hollywood is wrong when it portrays the winner as always getting the girl. In real life, the girl goes to the clever fellow who stays behind and comforts her while the Neanderthals roll around in the street.

· *9 February 1985* ·

An extremely restless night. My Swatch tells me it's only 6 a.m., so I stay in bed, feeling the butterflies churn in my stomach as I think about Munemann and his threat. Herr Munemann will probably make his move during gym. Which makes it imperative that I don't get caught in my tiny vestibule while I'm handing out the shorts and sneakers. Munemann has eighty pounds on me plus a vicious streak that I'm told would make a Shiite gunman green with envy. He is also thoroughly experienced in close combat. My only chance is to spear him with the broom handle and then pray. With my luck, I'll probably kill him, become the hero of D-block and spend the rest of my days in the hole.

Fear breeds a dangerous kind of solipsism. When Jerry the Scot asks me at breakfast for an old newspaper, I refuse, God knows why. I guess scared cats are selfish ones. When I return to my cell after getting my morning tea, I notice the snow. Thick snow, beautiful snow, the kind Gstaad sees all too seldom. I have two hours to go before gym time, but I cannot concentrate on a book today, not with Munemann's impending visit. So I day-dream about Gstaad when it snows and try to imagine what all my friends are up to this morning.

Well, at 7.30 a.m., none of my friends is up to anything.

Zographos has probably finished playing backgammon a couple of hours ago and the Green-Go is closed for the night. The one man sure to be awake is my old friend Angelo, the head waiter of the Eagle Club.

The Eagle is situated on top of the Wassengrat mountain, Gstaad's highest peak. Angelo sleeps in the club throughout the three-month winter season, coming down only occasionally to visit his wife who travels there from nearby Italy. Needless to say, Angelo's marriage is rock-solid, something that cannot be said about the marriages of many of the members, William Buckley being an exception. Angelo has been running the club since its inception in 1957. Its express purpose is to protect members from rubbing shoulders with the *hoi polloi* – poor people, ski bums and, I assume, convicts.

When in 1957 I arrived on the Gstaad scene, I was invited to join by the then president of the Eagle, the Earl of Warwick. It seems I was the first Greek he ever met who spoke English and his lordship was duly impressed. The day I paid my fee, however, I ran into a spot of bother. It had to do with the moonlight party the night before. These parties are made up of revellers taking the chairlift up the mountain at about eight in the evening, imbibing or, rather, decimating the Eagle's wine cellar and finally skiing down by torchlight.

On my first moonlight party, my friend John Zographos, the nephew of 'the man who broke the bank at Monte Carlo' – in reality, John's uncle owned the bank at Monte – had one of his typical bright ideas. He ordered Angelo to make three enormous cakes entirely of cream. The plan was to use the chef's creations as projectiles. Our target was Karim Aga Khan, recently enthroned as a living God and taking himself extremely seriously. (Well, there was also a girl for whose affections both the Aga and I were competing . . .)

Unknown to us, the Aga came to the party with an English diplomat, a rather common-looking chap whom we naturally mistook for one of the Aga's relatives. After a few drinks, we attacked. In a matter of seconds, both august figures were covered with cream.

The Aga, a prudent man, said nothing.

But the Brit took umbrage. He stormed over to our table and demanded an end to the hostilities. If memory serves, he used undiplomatic language, to say the least. In response, I threw another cake at him point-blank. That is when he grabbed my arm and flipped me over the table in a classically executed judo throw. As I was going over, however, despite my surprise at his most undiplomatic knowledge of that particular sport, I hooked his leg and brought him down with me. Zographos, running over to separate us, struck His Excellency's eye with his ski boot. It looked simply awful. Two Greek bullies against a poor diplomat.

Angelo tried to save the day by pointing out to Lord Warwick – who was less than pleased to see Her Majesty's representative looking as though he had put his face into a shredder – that the ambassador, after all, was not a member of the club, while Zographos and I were. It was a flimsy excuse, but that was 1957, civil servants were not taken too seriously, and the matter was resolved.

We were suspended for one year.

Of course, we apologized – grovelled would be closer to the truth – and now, twenty-eight years later, the ambassador, Zographos and I are fast friends. I can hardly say the same for the Aga.

Yes, pleasant memories do calm one down. Thinking about a cream fight so long ago somehow helps to make Munemann less chilling today. If only Zographos were in here with me, how much better I'd be feeling. And how much safer.

John Zographos is my oldest and best friend. I call him 'King Zog', after the last Albanian monarch, because he looks and acts like a sultan and is a prince in everything but name. He comes from an old and distinguished Greek family from which his uncle, Nico, escaped and went to Monte Carlo. Here he took over the bank at baccarat and challenged all comers. (He left a large fortune, mostly to my friend 'King Zog'.) Zographos is a playboy, spoiled and self-indulgent and lazy to the point of sucking in his stomach and letting his underwear drop rather than bending his knees to take it off. He is a legendary drinker, a gastronome of repute, generous as hell and the possessor of probably the biggest heart known to man.

Big, overweight and of dark complexion, he looks just like a Mediterranean monarch should. (Incidentally, he and King Farouk of Egypt were buddies and used to try to eat each other under the table.) Zographos loves to gamble and he loves women, drink and practical jokes, not necessarily in that order. We lived together for some twenty-odd years, going to nightclubs, chasing women, having a great time. Yet, if Yanni – 'John' in Greek – ever saw me taking drugs, he would call the fuzz right away. This is how adamant he is against what he calls 'the plague of the sixties'.

I met him for the very first time in a brothel. I was still under age, a not-so-sweet fifteen, and spending the summer with my parents in Greece. Back in those halcyon days, girls, especially Greek girls, did not go out on dates unchaperoned. Zographos was already known among our crowd as a man of the world, a big-spending, fun-loving aesthete, who frequented the most exclusive *maison de passe* of Athens. It was no secret among Athenian society that well-known politicians and rich industrialists were numbered among Madame Kiki's clients. Zog knew my old man and I decided to make use of their friendship. On the hottest day of the year – I remember it well because it was my birthday, 15 August – I figured the place would be empty, and Zog on the beach of some island with all the rest of the privileged Greeks. At three in the afternoon, I went down to Omonia Square and rang the bell on the bottle-green door. The place looked closed, but after a while a woman opened a window and asked me what I wanted. I lied and said that Mr Zographos had told me to wait for him there. 'Oh, all right,' she called down. 'He's upstairs.'

Needless to say, once I was inside my ruse was discovered, but Zographos was all smiles and understanding. 'Any son of John Theodoracopulos belongs in here,' was the way he put it, and he even treated me to you-know-what. As Captain Renault was once told by a certain Rick, it was the start of a beautiful friendship. It has endured to this day, it will until death.

Zographos married in 1982, a marvellous half-British, half-Greek girl, but I missed his wedding because I was covering the Falklands conflict in Argentina. But my little girl stood up for me and my little boy was a page. These days, Zog has cut down on the excesses of the past, but he remains a practical joker and a wonderful friend, a joy to be with. He has yet to do an honest day's work, but he is serene and happy, and a help to many not as lucky as he. I think of him, and then of Munemann, and I return to reality.

When I hear the screw about to unlock me, I take a last look around my cell and greet him like a long-lost friend. Then I head for the end of the landing where Mr Leggett is waiting to take us to the gym.

I start handing out shorts and sneakers, keeping my eyes and ears open for Munemann, but the beast is nowhere in sight. After handing out the equipment, I wander over to Mr Leggett and ask him if the class is complete. 'If you're worried about Munemann, he's not coming in just yet,' Leggett tells me with a knowing smile. 'He's in the block and will stay there for a while.'

What can one say when the mysterious hand of fate kindly lifts the heavy stone from one's chest?

All the sleeplessness, the butterflies, the fear, all for nothing. Munemann, it seems, got caught red-handed with some drugs and was thrown in the punishment block for at least a week. But I'm surprised that Leggett knew about Munemann's blackmail, his threats. How, I've no idea, but Leggett's knowing smile said a lot. Grasses (informers) are ten a penny in prison. That is how some inmates get more tobacco and even drugs from screws. Give away some useful information about what is going on and life is made easy for you. Although in the prison hierarchy a grass is on a par with the child-molesters, I must admit to feeling great relief that a warden was aware that Munemann had given me twenty-four hours to come up with what he wanted, or else. That 'else' being a blade in the belly, Mr Munemann's favourite reply to recalcitrant inmates.

I eat lunch with great relish. For once, the mashed potatoes and sponge cake taste good. I have one week to relax and think of pleasant matters.

· *11 February 1985* ·

A note from my father's office to say that my flat has been burgled. Sitting in a cell, surrounded by crooks and miscreants, this news strikes me as almost hilarious. The secretary who has written to me assures me that nothing of great value was taken, just my television and hi-fi, and my dinner jacket. I try to imagine what kind of person would steal a TV as well as a dinner jacket, and conclude that he must have been confused by the dark, mistaking my jacket for a zoot suit. This is the third time I've been broken into. The first was while I lived in Mayfair. All my sports trophies were stolen. Also a blue suit. The second time, in my present flat in Knightsbridge, only cash disappeared. That was obviously an inside (by an acquaintance, acquaintances?) job as whoever it was knew exactly where I kept my money. This time, I'm told, the trophies – which are silver-plated replicas – were left behind. Some discerning thieves know all about real and phoney silver.

When I tell an old-timer in the gym about the theft, he says that if they didn't take anything of value, it means that they – or he, or she – were looking for something in particular. But what? Or else, the old-timer suggests, someone was trying to plant something, a listening device perhaps. But I doubt it. There's been a lot of publicity about me lately, and some wise guy probably thought he'd find millions lying around. It's annoying, but I can't help it, it makes me laugh. Nothing like being robbed while in prison.

The second letter is from Archie Stirling and his wife, Diana Rigg, the actress. Archie, an old buddy, has written a funny epistle about Greeks being picked on by the English Establishment, of which he's certainly a member. Archie's father, Bill Stirling, and his uncle, Colonel David Stirling, were both heroes during the Second World War, fighting behind the German lines in the Libyan desert. There was a film about their exploits called *Play Dirty*.

Then a short note from Alexandra saying that Tom and Sheila Wolfe had called to offer their support. The great Tom had already rung me while I was waiting for my appeal, a kindness I shall not soon forget. (Ditto Bill Buckley, who, like most Conservatives, has been lashing out against the drug culture from the start.) Like all large talents, Tom is supportive of lesser ones. And he's no prima donna. He is as kind and considerate and gentle in his dealings with people as his literary style is precise and devastatingly accurate.

He and his wife and their two children live across the street from us in Southampton, but they prefer a quiet life and I don't see much of them. But I treasure their friendship. Last year, when a collection of my stories was published, I was embarrassed to ask him to write the foreword, but ask I did, and Tom's glowing preface made me out to be the freshest new talent since Tolstoy. The publisher, who knew better, featured his name more prominently than mine, and the book sold well. In fact, it got to be second on the East coast's bestseller list, which proves that Tom's moniker can sell anything.

I like everything Tom has ever written, but my favourite remains his demolition job on the 'radical chic' of Mr Bernstein's cocktail party. Two men in that piece stuck in my mind and, surprisingly, I came into contact with them both in 1972. The first was 'Field Marshal' Donald Coxe, as one of the chief thugs of the Panthers called himself, the other, Manhattan art dealer Richard Feigen, desperately asking the throng how to go about giving a party for the cop-killers.

In the winter of 1972, I went to Algiers for the *National Review* and did a story about the political exiles from America. It started as a serious piece, but eventually turned out to be a send-up of those miserable souls who found out much too late that being hunted by the police in America is still better than being free in Algeria. Donald Coxe, whom I interviewed while over there, was the worst of them all. A braggart, a liar and a pathetic sort of tough guy, he tried to intimidate me into giving him some money. When I told him I only had South African rands on me, he got all happy and ready to receive. It was a joke, of course, but Priscilla Buckley did put my story on the cover.

That summer, I was in the Hôtel du Cap in Antibes, and whom did I find occupying the next cabana but Mr Richard Feigen. As luck would have it, on the very first day, Gianni Agnelli arrived on his boat, dropped anchor and came over to my humble abode to chew the fat. Feigen looked at the Fiat chairman the way a hungry dog looks at a very large and very juicy bone. After Gianni left, Baron Heini Thyssen, or 'Europe's richest man', as the gossip columns refer to him, paid me an impromptu visit, and, to finish off the evening, a couple of the Niarchos kids came by. Feigen, watching all these incredibly rich cats coming and going, probably thought he had died and gone to heaven. Here was this Greek hack to whose cabana these fat cats were drawn like moths, and Feigen had the whole summer ahead of him to make the hack's acquaintance. Which he did almost immediately.

Mind you, he did more than that. In no time at all, he came up with the proverbial offer I could not refuse. It had to do with my selling his art to my friends. Refuse it I did, however, although I was very polite about it. What I recall best is the look he gave me, after my refusal. The kind of contemptuous stare you give to someone who has passed wind in a crowded elevator. I am glad to say I have never seen Feigen again.

· *15 February 1985* ·

Trevor is the first to tell me that a young con, about to be released, hanged himself the night before in C-wing. Trevor hates the police as well as the screws, so I don't believe him at first, but then in the gym the Yank from C-wing confirms it. This is the second inmate to take the easy way out since I've been in here. And with two days to go before release, too. The drug dealer facing forty years I understand, but this one sounds like a 'nutter', which is what we prisoners call our fellow convicts who are not altogether there.

Poor boy. I wonder what hell he must have gone through to do this, or, perhaps, what hell he was about to face. I ask a couple of guards about him, but not one of them will volunteer anything. Everyone, however, has heard about the suicide by the time dinner is served at mid-day and the rumours are flying fast and thick. Not surprisingly, it's blamed on the screws. I ain't so sure. Apparently, the young con was neither a troublemaker nor was he facing other charges upon release. Very mystifying. Very depressing.

By tea time, the rumours have subsided and everyone is talking about Aids. It seems there is an outbreak in Chelmsford prison and it has been hushed up. Lee once told me that, when he was in the hospital, some cons were suspiciously ill and the male nurses were taking precautions. I worry about it because my legs are cut from freestyling with Lee, and I have an open wound on the bottom of my foot. Shower slippers are not allowed in Pentonville. I wonder if the virus can live in hot water.

Frank Heavy tells me that, for the moment, there's nothing to worry about. The rumours started because a con from A-wing wrote to his mother and told her he had Aids. He knew the censors would read it and hoped they would send him home. It didn't work, says Frank, but they did test the con and found him healthy. It's good to hear, but I'm not convinced. Sleep comes late and the dreams are terrible.

· *17 February 1985* ·

Trevor Middleton, the Muhammad Ali look-alike, has been bugging me all week, asking for money and cigarettes, and making a face when I refuse. But no matter how much he grumbles, there is no way he can make me feel guilty. In here, we're all the same. What I possess, I've earned. I'm not about to give it away.

This morning, while we wait for Mr Leggett to march us to the gym, I tell Trevor about Mr Nakabayashi, who used to be the judo instructor at the New York Athletic Club and then moved to California to spread the faith to those laid-back types during the late sixties. He died of malnutrition while out there because he was too proud to ask his employer for a raise.

And this during the time when peace, love and brotherhood were what everyone in that great state was talking about . . . No one seems to have noticed that Sensei Nakabayashi wasn't earning enough to feed himself. There he was, in his late fifties, teaching diligently all day and throwing people around who were half his age and double his size, until one night he went back to his rented boarding-house room, lay down and died. Like a true samurai, he never once complained.

The gentleman who succeeded him at the NYAC, Mr Matsumura, has been my teacher for a long time and is made of the same stuff. Once he let slip that the worst

pain he'd ever felt was hunger pangs, but he never elab-
orated further. Proud people, the Japanese. As far removed
from my Pentonville brethren as, say, Mozart from the
Sex Pistols.

Of course Trevor is not impressed. He laughs and calls
my *sensei* dumb. I don't entirely blame him. Self-discipline
and self-control must seem awfully dumb to ghetto children. They know little about either quality. That's why the
rejection of authority and hard work has become the status
quo of the ghetto. Don't their social workers tell them
different?

After gym I open my mail and find a note from the
censor attached to one of my letters. 'This friend of yours
must have been smoking exotic cheroots while writing to
you,' reads the note and I laugh out loud, especially as the
letter comes from Chuck Pfeifer. Sure enough, the censor
– whom I've never met but feel I know well – is right. The
eighteen handwritten pages I find make absolutely no
sense, but then, most of the time, neither does Chuck.

Captain Chuck Pfeifer won two silver stars for bravery
in Nam as a Green Beret, which included a night-time
jump behind enemy lines from a chopper hovering at six
hundred feet. A West Point graduate, he now lives in
New York and produces commercials. His wife left him at
about the same time my first wife left me, and for the
same reasons. He and I have raised a lot of hell together,
the only difference being he likes big blondes and I sweet
young things. Pfeifer does not suffer from undue humility.
As he himself likes to say, and in the loudest possible
voice, 'I am a cultural hero. If I hadn't been born, F. Scott
Fitzgerald would have invented me.'

Good old Chuckie. I miss him, but his bragging would
get him nowhere in this hellhole. Cons are the greatest
braggarts I know.

The other letter was forwarded to me from home.
It's from Mr Marcial, my old Spanish teacher at Blair
Academy, the school I finally graduated from after both
Lawrenceville and Salisbury had given up on the little
Greek jailbird-to-be. Not that Blair was a breeze. On the
contrary. But Mr Marcial stuck by me and encouraged
me and in the end I did OK. I won something like ten
varsity letters, which was a record of sorts, was elected
captain of the soccer team and was a prefect of my house.
Reading his letter, I realize he doesn't know I'm in jail
and I feel the kind of shame I felt long ago, when I was
caught copying from a boy at the next desk, but was let
off because the equation I had copied he had got right
and I, somehow, wrong.

· *20 February 1985* ·

Today is visitors' day, and Anne Somerset, the talented historian daughter of the Duke of Beaufort, Alexander Chancellor, my old boss at the *Spectator*, Didi Saunders, a good friend, and Nigel Dempster, known in the gutter press as the 'Greatest Living Englishman', or GLE, are already seated as I'm led in after yet another humiliating body search.

Nigel is a hell of a fellow. He's known among the hacks as the GLE because although of English extraction he is an Australian, a fact the Brits won't let him forget. Dempster, you see, is a snob, but in the best sense of the word. He is also the greatest gossip columnist in the world, with many political and financial exclusives to his credit, and he heads an army of tipsters and informers that Lavrenti Beria would kill – no pun intended – for. He is married to the late Duke of Leeds's daughter and they've got a wonderful little daughter, Louisa. Dempster lives like the gentleman he is, and has managed to accomplish all this on his own after failing miserably at his first job – as a waiter in New York's El Morocco.

Unlike Suzy, the New York-based gossip whose style can only be described as arse-lickin' good, Dempster reports on foul play among the high and mighty, a dangerous business in a land where writing that someone was a bit under the weather can land you with a six-figure libel bill. His is what a gossip column is, or should be, all about. In New York, my two favourite 'diarists' are Liz Smith and Richard Johnson, of the *Daily News* and *New York Post* respectively. Both of them do a lot of sleuthing and neither of them will take the word of PR hacks as the Sermon on the Mount.

Gossip columnists have a bad name in England, especially with the upper classes, but in America, they're not only taken very seriously, they're also fawned upon by the social climbers that get mentioned in their columns. The smartest of all, needless to say, is John Fairchild, the owner of *Women's Wear Daily* and *W*, who created what we now refer to as 'Nouvelle Society'. Like a modern-day Napoleon, Fairchild promotes and demotes his creations at will, alternately blessing and cursing his marshals. But unlike the rest of us, he doesn't take his creations seriously and never mixes with them in polite company, as they say.

No sooner do I sit down with my friends than Nigel starts the needling, telling me how well-dressed I am for a change and how fortunate for me that I have lost weight without having had to pay for it. But the visit is cut short by a rude screw before my allotted time, and certainly before I have a chance to hear any of the latest gossip.

As on the previous visiting day, a deep depression settles in the moment I get back to my cell. Once again in solitude, I have time to think of the outside world and what normal life is like.

· *21 February 1985* ·

While lined up for the morning grub, the Yank from C-wing approaches and tells me that *Private Eye* has an outrageous piece explaining how I have bribed the warders to let my mistress spend the night with me in the 'ville'. This news does for my appetite what the Gulag Archipelago did for winter sports in the Soviet Union. I feel angry and frustrated, but most of all I worry that the powers that be might believe this bullshit and move me from my cell.

Richard Ingrams, the editor of the scandal sheet, is someone I used to lunch with frequently when I contributed a political column called 'Letter From'. One day Ingrams asked me to provide dirt about John Aspinall and Jimmy Goldsmith, two good friends. When I flatly refused, he began a campaign of vilification, going so far as to say in print that I was a child-molester.

He's a very strange man, this Richard Ingrams. Now in his early fifties, tall and pock-marked, he used to drink heavily until he went on the wagon for good. He detests everyone and everything, writes the most horrendous things about people, yet plays the cello every Sunday in his village church. He hates most, however, those who drink and chase women, as well as minorities, Jews and 'homosexualists', as he calls them, although his father, now dead, was rumoured to be the greatest closet queen since Dickie Mountbatten.

Back in 1979, Ingrams had me visit him in his country cottage for one night. There I met his wife, Mary, and his two children, Fred and Jubby. I liked them. The next day, we attended the Cheltenham races and after a long and good lunch I returned home. But before leaving I gave Mary Ingrams a fifty-pound note, asking her to put it in the bank so that when Jubby was older she could buy a pony with it. Like all girls of that age, twelve, Jubby was horse crazy. Mary thanked me and that was that.

I did not mean to be flashy or to impress them with my generosity, but simply to show my appreciation for their kind hospitality. Well, had I known what was to follow, I would have kept the root of all envy nice and folded in my pocket. Ingrams the misanthrope took my gesture as a ploy to eventually seduce his daughter and even went around saying as much to people who knew me. He did not get far, however. I later heard that many were outraged at the suggestion and showed it; some even threatened to sue him for slander. When Alexandra heard it, she hit the roof. She was all set to fly to London and confront him. I guess the fact he knew that I had gone on record saying I would never sue anybody made it easy for him to write such calumnies. Now he's once again hit below the belt, attacking me while I'm inside.

Having said that, I must ask the obvious question: Who am I to complain about hitting below the belt? I who say in print what I do? But I don't do what Ingrams does, and certainly not for his reasons. The best explanation I can offer for writing the way I do is that a righteous anger takes over when I perceive an injustice; it pushes and I tend to go over the top. Paradoxically, in everyday life I am reserved. I don't show my feelings. At family funerals,

I have cracked jokes, while during great emotional upheavals I've acted as though I were ordering a hamburger.

I like to excuse my kind of writing on the grounds that
we innocent targets receive random blows daily in the
form of appalling insults to our intelligence, dealt by the
media, by advertisers and by our politicians. Newspapers
and magazines wipe our faces in their endless puff pieces
about the people who run our towns not entirely for our
benefit and about those who make a comfortable living
out of screwing their fellow man. But yet another lesson is
learned in Pentonville Prep today. It is not much fun to
read horrible lies about oneself, especially when one cannot
answer back.

· *23 February 1985* ·

Munemann has suddenly come into the gym and has lined up for shorts and sneakers. My heart skips a beat, but when his turn comes he's all sweetness and smiles. Either he's setting me up or the block has taught him some manners.

This is Slim's last day in the slammer. Slim is a 5′7″, 250-pound blob, nothing but quivering flesh and cowardice. During basketball games he stands underneath the basket yelling for the ball and when somebody finally throws it to him, the opposing side sits down and lets him try to score. Although I've been the gym orderly for more than two months now, I have yet to see him put the ball through the rim. He is so uncoordinated that at times he falls down while standing still. He specializes in stealing cars and selling them for a fraction of their value. Needless to say, he finds a lot of buyers, but he also gets caught a lot. This is his ninth or tenth stretch. Mr Heavy tells me that the last car he stole was his father's and Slim's old man gave him away.

Today Mr Heavy warns him that the next time he comes in – which everybody thinks will be in the very near future – he will have to do fifty push-ups or go to the block. Slim laughs and everyone applauds. Extremely dirty, wearing glasses so thick I can almost see the details of the moon, Slim is somehow a lovable character. The dark side, though, is that he's reputed to be a stool-pigeon. I shall miss his basketball virtuosity.

· 25 February 1985 ·

Eddie Hayes, an American lawyer friend of mine, has come to visit. Lawyers do not have to be invited and can drop in at will. But Eddie has flown over for an express purpose. British lawyers are under oath not to carry anything out of prison, but foreign lawyers are not. I have asked Eddie, through Alexandra, to sneak out my diary, which I have been keeping by writing between the lines of the letters I've received. During cell searches, the screws have not even come close to looking inside the envelopes, but I'm getting nervous that they might, especially as Scanlon has it in for me.

Hayes is the personification of the American success story. He's an Irish Catholic from the Bronx, his father was a drunk, and he put himself through college and law school. He went to Virginia, where he joined the honorary society Tilka, but, hearing him speak, you would never think it. He talks 'Toity-toid Street' and all that, and when I – as another member of another honorary society at Virginia – wondered how anyone with such an accent could be asked to join, it broke the ice and we became fast friends.

Today he gives me all the New York news. Then we embrace and he leaves with my diary safely inside his shoe. When I tell him there is no search for lawyers, he says he's Irish, so in his case they may make an exception. I go back to the gym feeling relieved and happy.

*

Days are getting longer and longer, literally. When I look out of my tiny cell window, I can still see the grey sky at tea time, 4.30 p.m. It feels much like the end of a school term. Gate fever getting worse and worse.

· *27 February 1985* ·

This may sound like a Hollywood ending, but my hunch to send out the diary was certainly lucky. Just after gym this morning the assistant governor calls me in and tells me that I will be released early for good behaviour. As early as the day after tomorrow.

When you hear such news in prison, the reaction is the same as when you are first sentenced to go there. In an instant your whole life flashes by. Incredibly, I feel a sense of sadness. Of guilt. As if release will mean trouble. I tell Mr Heavy the news and he smiles knowingly. He and Mr Leggett and Mr Gordon have obviously had something to do with it. I almost break down, but instead I make some tea for them and then it's back to the old routine.

I say nothing to my mates because frankly I'm too ashamed. I'm getting out and they're staying behind. I'm going back to a life of ease, whereas if they ever get out, they will be going back to the ghetto. I make two exceptions, Warren and Pavlo. I'm going to leave them my extra clothes, the stuff I've stolen from the gym, things like extra shirts and socks, and also a radio, my watch, soap, toothpaste, food and four joints which were given to me by Tony the Loon long ago.

I make another exception, too, but covertly – the recipient will never know it. At lunch, once again Spiro asks for the truth about my outside life, my profession. 'Come on,' he says, 'no Greek waiter sounds like you.'

Finally I relent. 'All right, I'll tell you. I'm a head waiter.'

'Hah!' he explodes with satisfaction. 'I knew it!'

Later, I try to exercise, but my heart isn't in it. The inexplicable sorrow stays with me throughout the longest day.

· *28 February 1985* ·

An extremely restless night. By this time tomorrow, slopping out, prison food, life within a 13′ by 7′ cell, will be things of the past. And for some strange reason, I'm already feeling nostalgic.

They tell me that my reaction is common. POWs suffer from a sense of guilt, of failure, long after they are liberated. Perhaps I'm going through something similar, but I doubt it. POWs are honourable men who think being taken prisoner is proof of some individual failure or cowardice on their part. Once free, their torment as prisoners is transformed into guilt.

This could hardly be the case with me. What is it, then? It makes no sense. I could understand it if once outside I'd have to worry about food and rent and heat. Not having to worry about money spoils many prisoners, giving them a security in jail they've never had before; but I came in spoiled. If anything, it must be that the best precondition for a happy release is to have somewhere to go and someone to love. But I've already had that and still managed to get into trouble. I guess my premature nostalgia for the nick stems from the fear that once outside I'll return to my wicked ways.

It's understandable. One becomes extremely selfish inside. Not in the sense of wanting a 'soft' prison, however. On the contrary. Just as warders try to keep distant from prisoners and think of them as 'bodies', simply to forget they are fellow human beings, so do cons elect to return to prisons that conduct harsher regimes. A 'soft' prison only makes for missing the outside so much more. As I felt during the Christmas holidays and during outside visits. It's too much like pretending that you're outside, like faking freedom. It's dangerous. It unmans you. The only way to survive in the joint is by recognizing and accepting your imprisonment twenty-four hours a day.

After dinner I am taken down to A-wing, where a senior officer formally informs me about my release. Then he gives me a guideline, rules about what I am not allowed to do for the next three to five years, like shooting, for example. I crack a joke about a friend of mine – a notorious bad shot who's a danger to the community – being more deserving of that restriction, when Scanlon suddenly appears from nowhere and tries to have me sent to the block for insubordination. But the releasing officer resists and finally Scanlon goes away.

A little later, a warder comes to my cell, screams at me for its filthy condition and then whispers that Alexandra is already on her way over from America and will be waiting for me at home. Mr R. was smart to fake that scene. If it's found out that he's carrying messages, or having anything to do with a prisoner outside his normal duties, he may well lose his pension. The prison system in England comes down as harshly on warders as it does on cons. There is no hanky-panky and absolutely no bribing the screws.

When I think that in America inmates can make telephone calls at will, have all-day television and, weather permitting, outdoor sports, and that they enjoy the greatest luxury known to man – private toilets – I understand why the crime rate is so high over there. Over here, fifteen years from the year 2000, the toilet is still considered a luxury item. When the cells are unlocked in the morning, few buckets are emptied. Prisoners prefer to wrap up their filth in a piece of paper and throw it out of their window into the yard. It saves them the embarrassment of carrying their stinking buckets.

Coming to the end of one's sentence, however brief, is inspirational. It makes you want to summarize, to reach some kind of conclusion, to say something grand. Ironically, though, the more you try to think of that worthy conclusion or of something on that grand a scale, the more you realize that only fools or pompous left-wing pundits would do it. Let's face it, I had an easy time inside. A restful time, too. Prisoners, and in particular black prisoners, I found, have a victim-fixation complex, despite the absolutely objective treatment cons receive inside. No one, not even the worst recidivists I came into contact with, ever admitted to feeling guilty or to having been at fault. In prison, there is no spirit of community whatsoever. Everyone is out for himself. No drive for self-improvement, either, especially – and unfortunately – among the blacks. No one is ever cheerful, except for some homosexuals, which, it strikes me now, may justify the term 'gay'. Only two moods compete in prison – apathy and hostility. At bottom, everybody feels lonely yet craves solitude.

I stay up throughout the night, arranging and rearranging my few letters and notes. I don't care if they keep the letters, as they have the right to do, for the bulk of my diary is already out. Just before lock-up, I ask Mr Heavy to ask the governor if I may be allowed to leave from a side entrance since Mr Leggett, while entering the prison tonight, spotted a couple of photographers waiting outside.

They had done the same with George Best, the poor slobs. Waited for three days, but got the picture.

After lock-up, Mr Gordon and Mr Heavy come to say goodbye. I give them everything I have for Pavlo and Warren, and they let me out and take me to their cell to say goodbye. Warren breaks down and cries, sobs in fact, but Pavlo is as tough as ever. 'Get your yacht ready,' he says in front of the warders. 'I'll be out soon and I want to pay a little visit to Beirut.' I get his wife's address and tell him I'll take care of her when I'm on the outside. Spiro, too, starts to bawl, but his is bullshit.

Just before 6 a.m., I hear the one jingle of keys I've been waiting to hear since 14 December of last year. Mr Jones smilingly asks me to follow him out. As I pass Pavlo's and Warren's cells, I sense them up and listening. I knock and once again say goodbye. 'Good luck, have fun,' they yell back. They were wide awake. It is very hard to feel happy under the circumstances.

Once in the processing room, I am given my grey single-breasted suit, my black shoes, striped tie, blue shirt and signet ring, fifty pounds, courtesy of Her Majesty, and told to step right out as a free man. Mr Gordon is waiting in the yard and he takes me to a side entrance. He opens the door, looks out and waves me on. It is 7.33 a.m. and I am free.

· *Epilogue* ·

With the first whiff of freedom came an attack of paranoia. I felt sure that people in the street were looking at me. I window-shopped and walked slowly down the Caledonian Road. I wasn't keen to go home right away. I wanted to savour the feeling of being free to go and do as I pleased. But the gloom persisted.

Not for long. Suddenly a taxi screeched to a halt and two friendly faces appeared at the window. Next came two hands, beckoning me in. Then the window lowered and out floated two voices. 'Come on, hop in, we know you've been out all night . . .' It was Michael Medwin, a film producer and fellow member of the Turf Club, and the actor Albert Finney. Neither of them had a clue as to where I'd been, but when I told them they grew even more convivial and insisted I go with them for a drink. I declined. Their attitude, however, cheered me no end.

Eventually I hailed a cab and went home, where Alexandra gave me the first and nicest kiss I'd had in four months. Then I went to lunch at the Ritz with Richard Sykes, the lawyer who had stood by me throughout, and not long after that to dinner at Claridge's with Charles Moore. The atmosphere at both places was sedate, to say the least.

It is strange, but even Hollywood gets it right on this point. You don't go for the bright lights on the first night out of jail. Those in the know – to call them 'insiders' might be too corny a pun – advise you to take it easy during the first week. Not that I felt like painting the town red. On the contrary, when some friends rang to invite me to a party the next day, I feigned illness. I was much too embarrassed to be seen living it up, especially in merry old England. So the next morning Alexandra and I flew to Switzerland, where the children were waiting for us in Gstaad. The news had got out and the staff of the Palace Hotel lined up in the lobby and greeted me like the conquering hero I wasn't. I was very moved.

That evening Bill Buckley and his son Christopher gave a large dinner party intended to welcome me back to the lawful world. At the last minute I got cold feet and phoned Christopher, who along with being one of my closest friends was also my best man when I married Alexandra. He dismissed my fears by reminding me that I would be among people who liked me. 'Besides,' he said, 'having cavorted so brazenly in nightclubs just before you went in, it is ludicrous to be ashamed now that you have paid your debt to society.' Then he went on to tell me with his typical facetious wit how eager they all were to meet someone who for three months had been the guest of the Queen of England.

Bill's wife Pat was in New York, so Christo's recent bride, Lucy Gregg, was acting as hostess in place of her mother-in-law. Lucy is the daughter of Donald Gregg, a top CIA agent who spent thirty years in deep cover and is currently US ambassador to South Korea. He is an unsung hero, at least to this jailbird.

Trouble, though, seemed to be stalking me. As soon as I arrived at the Château de Rougemont, the Buckley winter abode, a weird accident happened. Roger Moore, the actor and long-time Gstaad resident, walked smack into a door and knocked himself out cold. Later I heard that he had

just turned to tell his wife to cool it – she was saying
something about prison, a taboo subject for that evening –
and thus failed to see the low beam before him. So, while
first aid was being hurriedly administered to James Bond,
I slipped into the room without fanfare. Christopher was
convinced I had done a 'dirty' on poor Roger. 'One of
your new prison tricks, I suppose.'

The group Bill had assembled did not exactly resemble
the crowd I'd left back at Pentonville. There were John
Kenneth Galbraith, Alistair Horne, Prince Romanov,
Barnaby Conrad III, Sam Vaughan, an assortment of
Scandinavian royalty and some Swiss ski instructors,
friends of ours of long standing. Professor Galbraith was
among the first to engage me in conversation, something
he had not often initiated in the twenty-odd years I had
known him. Later on in the evening, Bill told me how
Galbraith had recently done more for me than simply start
our idle chitchat that night.

Among the things I had neglected to do before my trial
was to resign from the Eagle Club. The truth is, I plumb
forgot. I have always thought of the Eagle as a glorified
place to lunch, not as a gentleman's club. So while I was
elsewhere, paying my debt to society, a Belgian multi-
millionaire, Louis Franck – since deceased – began a movement to drop me as a member. Although his efforts came
to naught, a letter sent in response on my behalf from the
good professor did cause an uproar. Galbraith, who has
consistently refused to join the Eagle, wrote that 'since
half of the membership of the club belongs behind bars, it
is unfair to pick on Taki'.

Still, despite the congenial atmosphere and the marvellous Buckley wine, the old spark wasn't there that night at
the dinner table. I was nevertheless extremely grateful to
Bill for his show of solidarity when I most needed it.

I stayed in Gstaad for a while, spending time with the children, but even there I felt awkward. My little girl was suspicious about where I'd been – she's smart and the invented job in Australia hadn't convinced her – and finally I had her mother tell her the truth. I myself wasn't brave enough. When I returned to London, I stayed away from the bright lights and saw only close friends like John and Aliki Goulandris, Harry Worcester and Oliver Gilmour.

After a few months, Alexandra decided after all to stay with me, the devil she already knew so well, and we have remained close and happy ever since. My mentor, Ernest Van Den Haag, had a lot to do with my redemption. His advice was simple. 'If you do it, don't brag about it,' was all he said, and, as always, he turned out to be correct.

Yet something was wrong. I still felt imprisoned. A lot of that had to do with the lie I'd told my father about my bust. Then, as weeks and months went by, the lie took on gigantic proportions in my mind. It was far greater than a lie. It was the very essence of immorality. At least, according to my own beliefs, where immoral behaviour lies not in the hot flame of desire but in the masking of truth for profit. In fact, the lie was worse than that. I was betraying my old man by pretending to myself that I was shielding him from pain, the pain of bad news; when actually I was worried about what he might do if he knew the truth. Alexandra was also deeply troubled by my fakery. Nevertheless, I chose to live the lie; until 14 July 1989, to be exact, the day he died.

Another constant irritant was the writing of this book. In reviewing horror stories, critics say that the more human the monster, the greater the character created. While I was in Pentonville, I was certain I would write a masterpiece once free. Needless to say, this was not happening. While inside, I dreamed of turning the dry facts of my diary into a lyrical *tour de force*, describing the 'monsters' well enough to make them unforgettable characters. I guess this is only human. Prison, as places of torment do, sharpens the image. Once outside, however, humility, reality and a sense of the ridiculous take over, and prison solipsism turns into embarrassment.

The following year I was back in court, but a civil court this time. A woman had sued the *Spectator* and me for libel. Rosemarie Marcie-Riviere, a Swiss national, was a five-times-married septuagenarian who made Zsa-Zsa Gabor seem a wilting flower by comparison. Lasting two weeks, the case drew huge crowds and publicity. The papers called it the best show in town for the entire month of June. But, for once, it was good PR. We lost, but our adversary, the social-climbing Madame Marcie-Riviere, won a Pyrrhic victory. The quality newspapers disagreed with the verdict and *The Times* went so far as to describe me as a moralist writing essays under the guise of gossip.

The fifteen-million-dollar suit brought against me by Richard Golub was thrown out of court and then thrown out again on appeal. *Esquire* and I were brilliantly defended by Victor Kovner, who insisted there was something very wrong with a system that allows such frivolous suits even to be heard. Golub had flown to London to testify against me as a character witness in the Riviere case, but my barrister had turned the tables on him by 'suggesting' – the British term for accusing one in court – that Golub 'was suffering from impotence and a persecution complex, pressing the point so far, in fact, that the judge took pity on him and cut the cross-examination short. The last I heard of Golub, he had sued his wife Marisa Berenson for money during their divorce, but there, too, he had failed to win a penny. I hear his social climbing has also hit a snag.

Shortly thereafter, I was forcibly retired from the national karate team because of my age. I was replaced as captain by the best *karateka* ever to come out of Greece, my former student Dimitri Kazakeas. He and I continue to train often and, although I have lost speed and power, I think I'm still improving.

Then, in September 1987, while swimming from my father's boat off the island of Spetsai, I felt a sharp jellyfish bite on my chest. Or so I thought. That evening I felt nausea and a fierce ache just below my breastbone, and I began to sweat profusely. My temperature went up. My father was furious and accused me of trying to kill myself by living it up every night. He ordered me to bed.

In the morning, after I'd had a terrible night, Daddy took one look at me and told the captain to steam back full speed to Athens. The doctor immediately diagnosed a heart attack and sent me to the hospital. Intensive care. As soon as the doctor would permit, I flew to London, checked myself into a clinic and had the balloon treatment to clean up my arteries. I have felt almost perfectly fine ever since.

In 1988, Nicky Kalo and I won the National Veterans Doubles without the loss of a set. It was strange, going back to the various Athens tennis clubs where he and I had lost but once during the last thirty years. We recognized only a few of the older members and were recognized by even fewer among the young. The game had certainly changed, or rather the people playing it had. They grunted when they hit the ball; almost everyone used foul language. The dress code suffered the most. The only tradition that has survived in tennis is the game itself, but its elegance and subtlety have definitely gone. For one, technology has overtaken it. The new high-tech racquets have changed the game for the worse. Everything is boom-boom, with lots of top spin but without finesse or touch. The game is far less interesting, just as race driving is. Once upon a time, a courageous player of inferior ability could beat his superior opponent through wile and sheer hard work. Ditto in race driving. But, with the ball being hit as hard as it is today, there's no chance for anyone lacking in brute power. A good comparison is baseball, where the major leagues use only wooden bats, while the pee-wee leagues are permitted to use aluminium. Thus the continuity in the level of play has been preserved, without the game being overpowered by technology.

But far worse has been the general attitude of the players. Money, of course, is partly to blame. Like those hotshot Wall Streeters, today's top stars seem to forget that the end does not justify the means. Jimmy Connors and John McEnroe, too, have a lot to answer for. Their example has been the worst I've ever encountered, so far as the younger players are concerned. Now we even have the ghastly showboat Agassi running around on court in what looks like his underwear, and pink underwear at that. His behaviour is as awful as his sartorial sense. Increased prize money, tiebreaks, best of three sets rather than five, and millions in endorsements have brought only complaints and more complaints from our stars, which makes me glad to be old and out of the whole mess.

Ever since my release, I have been asked many times to write and to comment on television about prison. I was imprisoned for too short a period to really qualify as a con, but the few times I have given my views in public, the so-called experts took offence. They disliked my opinions, even disparaged them. To put it succinctly, my view was, and still remains, that the liberal experiment of throwing restraint to the wind, of blaming society for

the crimes committed by habitual criminals,' of coddling
the perpetrators, resulted in an even bigger failure than
Communism. How fine and noble it is to preach that
inmates need to be given a sense of self-worth, not
humiliated and dehumanized! That society should deal
with the causes of crime before it is committed!
BUT HOW DO YOU ACCOMPLISH THESE LOFTY AIMS?

The vicious, the amoral and the violent are sent to prison
for three reasons: to protect the public from harm; to
punish those who threaten the maintenance of an orderly
and just society; to rehabilitate criminals, meaning, to
change their aberrant patterns of behaviour. The liberal
view elevates rehabilitation above the rest. Results show
that this preference is grossly misguided. I recently read an
article about New York City's toughest prison, Riker's
Island. Every inmate interviewed sounded like a sixties
radical. All of them talked about the failure of society to
provide adequate jobs and housing and education, exactly
as my friends at Pentonville did. Apparently, criminals
learn quickly how to parrot the jargon of the day. But
what else do they learn?

The Riker's Island inmates also groused about 'unsanitary conditions'. About toilets that didn't flush, about
showers that dripped instead of poured. About sometimes
having to stay in one cell for twenty-three hours a day.
Well, all that is the norm for Pentonville, though I had to
laugh when I read about toilets in the cells. And showers,
however defective.

The problem, of course, is complex to the point of absurd-
ity. How do we rehabilitate people who can't read and write?
Who are addicted to drugs? Who can make a living only by
hurting other people? Do we lock them up and throw the key
away? Yes, of course, what else is there to do? No, of course
not, how inhumane! What's the right answer? I haven't a clue.

One belief I do hold for certain, though, is that we should punish white-collar crime differently than we do. If white-collar criminals actually lost every penny they ever gained through fraud, and then some, very few would risk breaking the law. Sending white-collar criminals to country-club jails which we then have to pay for, amenities and all, is clearly no solution. It's even sillier than feeling guilty for the criminality of others. Ivan Boesky laughed all the way to the bank, as did Milken, as do most people who commit clever, non-violent crimes and fraudulently enrich themselves. Take away every penny from them, I say! Then see how many white-collar criminals remain.

Ironically, two recent cases that vaguely resembled mine raised the hackles of some liberals. The first concerned John Zaccaro, the son of Geraldine Ferraro the 1984 Democratic vice-presidential running-mate of Fritz Mondale. Zaccaro was caught red-handed selling – not buying – cocaine, and selling it to students, to boot. He pleaded not guilty, although everyone on the Middlebury College campus knew him as a drug dealer. He was given four months in one of those country-club prisons and his parents grumbled that young John was treated unfairly because of their renown. Zaccaro even enjoyed maid service in the police apartment complex where he did his brief time.

Now, what is an illiterate black youngster to think if the police arrest him for selling crack to kids and he gets three to five years? Zaccaro should have done hard time, no question about it.

Then there was the case of Bernard Farbar, convicted of selling a large amount of marijuana, enough to make him a wealthy man. Farbar had his day in court, but he had it once again in the pages of *Esquire*, which published his lengthy and lachrymose article in which he whined about the bad food, the stiff sentence – six years which could well have been twenty-five – and about how awful life inside Loretto truly is. (Loretto, incidentally, is considered a soft prison, not at all a full-blown penitentiary.) Farbar, however, had many friends among those who count. In fact, he was a groupie to writers and other celebrities, as well as being quite a capable writer himself. Along with Farbar's article, *Esquire* chose to print a letter from William Styron that cried out against a prison system he described as an American Gulag. Farbar was educated enough to know better, and Styron a hundred times more, making his comparison a bitter insult to those who suffered in the real Gulag – suffered for their beliefs, not for their greed. But such are the joys of liberalism.

Then, taking the opposite position from Styron's, are those who think that the only solution for habitual violent offenders is a penal colony, not as a punitive measure but as the logical consequence of their actions. Having seen career criminals up close, I tend to lean in that direction. If people wish to live in a brutal and lawless climate, why must the taxpayers bear the brunt? Penal colonies are run by the inmates themselves. They are self-sufficient. And they serve the purpose of allowing violent people to build a society in their own image. Mind you, I'm well aware that the first politician to offer this suggestion will be run out of town, even if the town is Palm Beach.

The *annus mirabilis* 1989 turned out to be the most monumental year since 1945. 1989 alone saw more change than most centuries, thus making the eighties what the sixties had tried and failed to become: the decade of change and freedom.

My one regret is that my father – who had predicted these events all along – did not live to see the great political upheavals take place. In the early hours of 14 July 1989, on his way to spend the weekend on his boat with some friends, he died of a heart attack. Yet he who had fought the 'evil empire' tooth and nail throughout his life would not have gloated. Brave men are magnanimous in victory and my father was probably the bravest man I have ever known. And also the most modest. He won the highest decorations for courage both on the battlefield and in civilian life, but he never talked about these honours nor did he ever wear his medals. A fearless businessman who thought everything possible, he never cut corners and he never cheated his competitors. And he employed people, thousands of them. He was not a greenmailer, he was not an arbitrageur, he was not a leveraged buyout artist.

When my mother rang me early that morning with the news – I was in London – I broke down for the first time in forty years. On the day of my father's funeral, the high and mighty all came – including the Greek Prime Minister – but so did many of the people who work, or had worked, for him. And also many ladies of the night. In fact, while I shielded my mother from seeing my father's body lowered into the family crypt, a young girl stepped forward and threw a single red rose on to his casket. It was par for the course. Then they closed the crypt and he was gone for ever.

Gone for ever ... I would be a liar if I didn't admit that, despite the numbing grief, I also felt the heady sense of emancipation course through me. Still, ever since his death, not a day has gone by when I have not thought of him. I dream of him regularly. I took over his various enterprises in Greece, but I've hardly been able to fill his shoes. In fact, I haven't. One stroke of good fortune, though, did come about: I made up with my brother. After my father's death, I extended a hand of reconciliation to him and he accepted it, a gesture he'd refused to make for thirty-odd years. My mother – like the great lady she is – has remained in deep mourning since her husband went to his grave.

On a brighter note, the *Spectator* continues to prosper under Conrad Black, the Canadian tycoon who bought the *Daily Telegraph*, the *Sunday Telegraph* and us. Charles Moore resigned as editor to write a novel, and his deputy, Dominic Lawson, now stands at the helm. Dominic is the third editor I am writing under and, of all my work anywhere, my column there gives me the most pleasure.

The demons are still with me, but now they seem heavily sedated. I look back at the past and both the good and bad times seem happy enough to me. Although Pentonville remains with me, always, I bear no scars. On the contrary. Dimitri Kazakeas thinks I'm much tougher since my incarceration. Perhaps I am.

Unlike a biography, a diary cannot tell the complete and unbiased story of a life. Biographies can't either, of course, but, freed from the concerns of the purely subjective, of the personal ego, they make a better stab at the truth. Diaries are quite another matter. I don't know how true a diary can ever be, no matter how some diarists long to spill everything and think they do. Still, what emerges willy-nilly is their truth, not *the* truth. My psyche absolutely forbids that. It will not permit me to tell the real truth, whatever that means. (All right, it means my truest fears and feelings, at least as they appear at the moment of writing.) Like many people, I have an instinctive horror of 'revelatory' books, the scourge of our era. I find myself increasingly embarrassed by an age that seems increasingly to be embarrassed at nothing. Where privacy is an antiquated notion.

So personal truths, how I suffered, how I felt, are useful only if they add to the book, not to personal dishonour. There is much about my private life I would rather die than tell. Despite the current trends in publishing, a diary at its best is not a sewer. Sinyavsky's *A Voice from the Chorus* is a perfect example. He ruminates, he describes and he tells enough for the reader to get a strong sense of the man, but *c'est tout*.

Anyway, writing that's inspired by a need for therapy is no good. So I hope that my diary here does not fall into the 'I am a man, I suffered, I was there' breed of prison memoirs. I have not included a list of suggested reforms, as these books usually do. As I mentioned several pages back, my prison experience has brought me to consider a number of questions about our penal system and our current social attitudes, but so far not one of these questions has led me to a single answer I can stand on. All I know with certainty is that I am a much stronger, happier man today and that, alas, Pentonville had something to do with it.

Or perhaps it's just old age creeping in.